THE ATLANTIC TELEGRAPH.

REPORT OF THE PROCEEDINGS

AT A

BANQUET,

GIVEN TO

MR. CYRUS W. FIELD,

BY THE

CHAMBER OF COMMERCE OF NEW-YORK,

AT THE METROPOLITAN HOTEL, NOVEMBER 15TH, 1866.

THE NEW YORK
PUBLIC LIBRARY
DUPLICATE
SOLD

JOHN W. AMERMAN, Printer, No. 47 Cedar Street, N. Y.

The

Chamber of Commerce of the State of New York.

Respectfully Invites

To Meet Mr. Cyrus W. Field At Dinner,
on Thursday the 15th inst. at Six O'clock P. M. at the Metropolitan Hotel,
to Exchange Congratulations on the happy result of his efforts in the great work of
Uniting by Telegraph the Old World with the New.

A. A. Low.		Jonathan Sturges.
George Opdyke.	Committee.	Stewart Brown.
Wm. E. Dodge.		Samuel B. Ruggles.

An early answer is requested.

New York, November 7th 1866.

THE success of the Atlantic Telegraph is one of the great events of the nineteenth century. History will point to it as one of the landmarks of modern progress. In 1858, on the morning after the landing of the cable at Valentia, the London Times said: "Since the discovery of COLUMBUS, nothing has been done in any degree comparable to the enlargement thus given to the sphere of human activity." What was then but little more than a gleam of the future, is now a permanent reality. To Americans especially is this of moment, as it brings the New World alongside the Old, and establishes a community of thought and intelligence between the two hemispheres. Hence they have watched its progress with deep interest, and also with pride, for the part in it borne by one of their countrymen, who was the foremost in the enterprise, who started it at the beginning, and stood by it to the end. The merchants of New-York, proud of the achievement of one of their own number, wished to do him honor. Accordingly the Chamber of Commerce appointed a committee to arrange for some suitable celebration of the final triumph of the Ocean Telegraph, which should also be a testimonial to its projector. After consultation, it was concluded that the best form it could take was that of a Public Banquet, as that would enable a large number of citizens to join in the demonstration, and in the congratulations of the hour. Accordingly, the following letter was addressed to Mr. FIELD:

Chamber of Commerce of the State of New-York,

New-York, October 15, 1866.

Dear Sir:

The undersigned, members of the Chamber of Commerce of the State of New-York, and in its name, desiring publicly to express their joy at the successful establishment of Telegraphic communication between the Old and New Worlds, and their warm congratulations to you upon the happy result of the enterprise to which you have devoted so many years of patient and intelligent labor, request your acceptance of a Banquet at an early day, that they may hear from your lips the story of this great undertaking, and extend to you in person their cordial greetings.

We are, dear Sir,

Your sincere friends,

A. A. Low,
George Opdyke,
William E. Dodge,
Jonathan Sturges,
Stewart Brown,
Samuel B. Ruggles,
Moses Taylor,
John D. Jones,
John A. Stewart,
Robert B. Minturn,
Charles H. Marshall,
Peter Cooper,
Robert Lenox Kennedy,
Wilson G. Hunt,
William H. Fogg,
Edwin D. Morgan,
Henry F. Vail,
Adam Norrie,
Alexander M. White,
Wm. Augustus White,
Alexander W. Bradford,
Moses H. Grinnell,
R. W. Weston,
George Griswold,
Eugene Kelly,
Paul N. Spofford,
Samuel D. Babcock,
Benjamin H. Field,
George W. Lane,
Alexander T. Stewart,
Horace B. Claflin,
John A. Stevens,
William G. Lambert,
Henry G. Stebbins,
W. F. Havemeyer,
John C. Green,
James Low,
Joseph A. Sprague,
William J. Beebe,
Charles E. Beebe,
James How,
C. V. S. Roosevelt,
Robert L. Stuart,
Thomas Suffern,
N. L. McCready,
Samuel B. Caldwell,
Charles S. Baylis,
Barnet L. Solomon,
Morris K. Jesup,
James Brown,
Stanton Blake,
Loring Andrews,
William Butler Duncan,
H. H. Van Dyck,
John J. Cisco,
Joseph Sampson,
Royal Phelps,
J. Pierrepont Morgan,
Marshall O. Roberts,
Lloyd Aspinwall,
Benjamin Aymar,
Norman S. Bentley,
Charles W. Burton,
Francis Baker,
Robert H. Berdell,
Charles Butler,
Demas Barnes,
E. Caylus,
William Chauncey,
William T. Coleman,
Joseph J. Comstock,
N. D. Carlile,
Joseph A. Dreyfous,
Henry A. Dike,
William A. Darling,
E. R. Goodridge,
William R. Garrison,
Joseph Gaillard, Jr.,

John Taylor Johnston,	Henry A. Smythe,	Frank E. Howe,
Marshall Lefferts,	Solon Humphreys,	Oliver Hoyt,
Frederick S. Winston,	R. H. McCurdy,	E. S. Jaffray,
Thomas Slocomb,	Elliott F. Shepard,	Charles G. Landon,
Henry Grinnell,	James Lorimer Graham,	Richard Lathers,
S. B. Chittenden,	George F. Thomae,	Erastus Lyman,
Jackson S. Schultz,	H. Dollner,	Charles H. Ludington,
James K. Place,	E. H. R. Lyman,	John Linnemann,
John S. Williams,	Josiah O. Low,	Marvin J. Merchant,
William H. Guion,	William A. Wheeler,	Henry E. Moring,
Henry K. Bogert,	George A. Fellows,	James M. Motley,
Arthur Leary,	M. R. Cook,	Joseph U. Orvis,
William E. Dodge, Jr.,	Levi P. Morton,	William H. Osborn,
Paul Spofford,	Edward F. Davison,	Isaac G. Pearson,
Thomas Rowe,	Elliot C. Cowdin,	Isaac N. Phelps,
Hugh N. Camp,	Abram Wakeman,	Daniel L. Ross,
Henry W. Hubbell,	Henry M. Taber,	George B. Raymond,
Sheppard Gandy,	A. S. Barnes,	Lewis Roberts,
William T. Blodgett,	Sinclair Tousey,	Henry F. Spaulding,
George W. Blunt,	William Orton,	Samuel Sloan,
George S. Stephenson,	Charles F. Loosey,	William H. Stiles,
Frederick A. Conkling,	E. A. Quintard,	Nathaniel Sand,
A. G. P. Stokes,	Jacob Wendell,	Martin Bates, Jr.,
Frederick Sturges,	S. H. Wales,	James M. Brown,
John T. Terry,	Robert T. Woodward,	Hiram Walbridge,
D. Van Nostrand,	William H. Webb,	Horace Gray,
A. R. Wetmore,	James M. Constable,	Wm. M. Vermilye,
James Wadsworth,	Leonard J. Stiastny,	Edward C. Donnelly,
George Cabot Ward,	George W. Dow,	John Riley.

To

Cyrus W. Field, Esq.

Reply of Mr. Field.

New-York, Oct. 30th, 1866.

Gentlemen:

I have the honor to acknowledge the receipt of your letter requesting my acceptance of a banquet to be given by the Chamber of Commerce of the State of New-York, to celebrate the completion of the Atlantic Telegraph.

Were I to consult my own feelings, I would avoid any public demonstration, and leave the Cable to speak for itself. But your invitation is so kindly expressed, and signed by so large a number of our most influential citizens, that I cannot refuse.

I accept, therefore, for the pleasure it will afford to meet so many friends; and also for the opportunity it will give to pay a deserved tribute to those who have taken part in this enterprise on both sides of the Atlantic.

With great respect, I am, Gentlemen,

Very truly your friend,

CYRUS W. FIELD.

To Messrs.

A. A. Low,
George Opdyke,
William E. Dodge,
Jonathan Sturges,
Stewart Brown,
Samuel B. Ruggles,
Peter Cooper,
Alex. T. Stewart,
Moses Taylor,
John A. Stevens,
Marshall O. Roberts,
Henry Grinnell,
Wilson G. Hunt,
John J. Cisco,
Edwin D. Morgan,
Joseph Sampson,
Jackson S. Schultz,
James Brown,
C. V. S. Roosevelt,
Henry A. Smythe,
Robert B. Minturn,
Moses H. Grinnell,
William T. Blodgett,
John C. Green,
William H. Osborn,
William H. Webb,
S. B. Chittenden,
and others.

The Banquet was given at the Metropolitan Hotel on the evening of the 15th of November. The occasion brought together a company of three hundred gentlemen, embracing a very large proportion of our most distinguished citizens—men eminent in every walk of life—bankers and merchants, clergymen and lawyers, and judges of the courts, authors, and artists, and editors, together with members of the government and foreign ministers, and officers of the army and navy. A list of the invited guests, who were present, is given in the Appendix.

At half-past six the company entered the hall.

Grace

Was said by the Rev. William Adams, D. D.

Father Almighty! Thee we acknowledge as the Maker of the Heavens and the Earth. The Sea also is Thine, and all that passeth through the waves thereof. Thou hast made of one blood all nations of men for to dwell upon the face of the earth, and hast determined the bounds of their inheritance. At all times we bless Thee for the gift of thy Son Jesus Christ, the one Redeemer of the human family, through whom we receive all that is profitable for the life that now is, and fulness of promise for the life that is to come. We render thanks to Thee for all arts and inventions by which the common welfare of the human race is promoted; and upon this occasion we desire devoutly to render thanks to Thee for the success with which Thou hast crowned the repeated endeavors of Thy servants and children in uniting together the hemispheres of our globe, so long separated by the great and wide sea; and as Thy favor and aid were invoked at the outset of this undertaking, so would we now, in Thy name, consecrate its success to all beneficent ends, to friendly commerce, to international peace, and growth and honor, and never may it be desecrated by one word of evil import. We implore Thy blessing upon all projects that look for the prosperity of nations and the progress of the world, even down to the time when the Son of Man shall come, according to His own word, "even as the lightning cometh out of the East and shineth unto the West," to reign in everlasting righteousness and peace and joy. All which we ask through Jesus Christ our Lord. Amen.

At nine o'clock Mr. A. A. Low, President of the Chamber, called the company to order.

INTRODUCTORY REMARKS OF THE PRESIDENT.

MEMBERS OF THE CHAMBER OF COMMERCE, FELLOW-CITIZENS AND FRIENDS: I suppose it is pretty well understood that the interest of this occasion will not depend upon any thing that proceeds from the chair. Nevertheless, it will be a relief to some of you to know thus early that your chairman appreciates the general sentiment in this regard, and will strive to be governed by it.

Through the courtesy of the committee charged with the arrangements for this entertainment, the duty has been assigned me of extending, in the first instance, a cordial welcome to all those distinguished guests who have come from far and near to grace our festive board; and, in the language of the card issued by the Chamber, "to exchange congratulations with Mr. CYRUS W. FIELD on the happy result of his efforts in the great work of uniting by telegraph the Old World with the New."

In the interest of good order, I am desired, in the second place, particularly to request of all who are before me a strict adherence to the schedule of regular toasts as they are announced by the chair. And, finally, let me ask for myself that measure of indulgence which is due to inexperience in your presiding officer, who is honored with this position because of his official relation to the Chamber, and not out of a paramount regard to the fitness of things--the adaptation of the man to the place.

Letters were then read, expressing regret for absence, from the President of the United States; from Chief Justice CHASE; from General GRANT; from Sir FREDERICK BRUCE, the British Minister; from Hon. CHARLES SUMNER,

Chairman of the Committee of the Senate on Foreign Relations, and from General DIX, our newly-appointed Minister to France. These are given in the Appendix, with letters from others which there was not time to read.

There was a telegraph instrument in the room, and despatches were received during the evening from Mr. SEWARD, Secretary of State, and other members of the Cabinet at Washington; from Lord MONCK, Governor-General of Canada; from the Governor of Newfoundland; from Capt. Sir JAMES ANDERSON, dated at London the same day; and from others. These were read later in the evening.

The President then gave the first regular toast, as follows:

The President of the United States—chief magistrate of thirty-five millions of people—bound in Union never to be broken.

Drank standing, the band playing "Hail Columbia."

The second toast:

Her Majesty Queen Victoria, of Great Britain, the constant friend of America—honored and beloved alike in our country and in her own.

Music, "God save the Queen."

On introducing the third regular toast, the President spoke as follows:

SPEECH OF A. A. LOW, ESQ.

GENTLEMEN: In the days of ancient Rome, when the armies of the Republic were extending her sway over all the surrounding countries, and her Generals returned from successful war, bearing with them the trophies of victory, it was their custom to halt outside the gates of the city and *demand* a triumphal entry! When this was granted by the Roman Senate, and adequate preparations had been made, they were received with demonstrations of applause—welcomed by popular acclamation.

Triumphal arches, erected two thousand years ago, still survive to attest the grandeur of earlier and later conquests, and with what imposing ceremonies the heroes of the republic and the empire were admitted to the capital.

So it has been in all times; and history is a continuous record of homage paid to military genius—however aggressive, however destructive of the rights and happiness of man.

Nor has the tribute of respect been confined to those who have gained success in war; nor has it been limited to kings and queens, or the commanders of victorious armies.

In all countries and in all ages, persevering, courageous, faithful and devoted men of every calling and condition of life, have been found to command the admiration of their fellows and reap the reward of well doing.

The sentiment which honored martial prowess in the days of ancient Rome exerts the same power, at the present time, over every American heart.

In our own day, with a simplicity more truly republican, but with an earnestness not less sincere than that of the Roman people, we welcome to our cities and our homes the victorious Generals, who by their valor and their success have re-established for ourselves and for our children the principles of liberty and good government throughout our land. Nor have we ever been backward in awarding to men of high position in the State, or to men distinguished as instructors and benefactors of the race, the honors that are justly their due. In days gone by it has been our pride and our pleasure to welcome with such civilities as we know how to render, those who have been raised to the highest office in the gift of the people, and alike the prince and the peer of other realms.

But we are not met here now to exalt president, potentate, prince or titled lord; albeit the friend in whose honor we *are* assembled, is known by a Christian name which seems to have been prophetic of his future renown as a king among men—and his chief title to our regard comes to us through a long line of descent; not that genealogical line, which, proceeding from father to son, can be distinctly traced—uniting family with family—but that line, which, descending from Valentia on the coast of Ireland, and stretching two thousand miles across the bed of the Atlantic to Newfoundland—reaches "Heart's Content"—uniting continent with continent—nation with nation—Europe with America—bringing all into the most intimate relations, and securing to each other instant knowledge of every thing that is of mutual concern. (Applause.)

We have met not to celebrate a victory of arms on land or sea, not the acquisition of conquered provinces, annexed to our national domain; but we have met, rather, to commemorate an event of vast international interest—an epoch in the progress of science—the attainment of a great commercial boon—a triumph over obstacles hitherto deemed insurmountable. We are met to celebrate an achievement that reflects much credit upon the handicraft of the mechanic, on the skill and capacity of the sailor, on the intelligence and liberality of the merchant, and elicits our admiration of the electricians who have artfully explored the occult laws of nature, and, seizing subtle powers hitherto but partially developed—have converted them to the use of man—giving him a new sense of what Omnipresence is.

We have come here to acknowledge the aid imparted to the Atlantic Telegraph Company by the Governments of Great Britain and the United States, through the enlightened action of their respective and intelligent statesmen; to own the important part taken by the naval ships of both countries; the generous pecuniary support rendered by the wealthy merchants and factors of Great Britain; and, above all, to recognise the goodness of the Divine Being who has crowned the labors of all with abundant success—who has vouchsafed such wonderful gifts to man! (Applause.)

It is related in the volume recently published from the pen of my friend, Rev. Dr. FIELD, who is here present, that in the year 1853, Mr. F. N. GISBORNE, who was then the chief officer of the Nova Scotia Telegraph Company, conceived the idea and entered upon the work of connecting "St. John's, the most easterly port of America, with the main continent."

After initiating a vigorous effort with the aid of other parties, he failed in this, and coming to New-York, sought the ear and the interest of Mr. CYRUS W. FIELD, who embarked with all his enthusiasm in the enterprise. Mr. FIELD summoned to his side PETER COOPER, MOSES TAYLOR, M. O. ROBERTS and CHANDLER WHITE, and on the decease of the last named, WILSON G. HUNT, and as counsellor and aid, his brother, DAVID DUDLEY FIELD. These representative men of our mercantile community grappled the undertaking with their accustomed energy, devoting to it time and money without stint. I need not dwell upon the details, for they are all matters of record. The arduous and costly work was accomplished. A road was cut through 400 miles of wilderness, and after two attempts in 1855 and 1856, a cable, procured in England, was laid across the Gulf of St. Lawrence. This done, Mr. FIELD, with the concurrence of his associates, embarked for England to secure needed co-operation in the plan—projected by him from the first—of extending the line across the Atlantic Ocean. Deep sea soundings had already been taken by Lieutenant BERRYMAN, of the U. S. Navy, and subsequently they were continued by Commander DAYMAN, of H. B. M. ship "Cyclops."

It soon became apparent that the larger enterprise could only or best be conducted under a charter, and with a new company to be formed in England. There experience in submarine telegraphy, skill in the manufacture of cables, pecuniary means and ability to cope with the difficulties of the undertaking, were at ready command.

The Atlantic Telegraph Company was formed with a capital of £350,000. In the division of the stock, Mr. FIELD claimed £100,000 for the United States, and was awarded £88,000, all of which he paid for in sterling money. It was an international enterprise, and he would have his countrymen share in the honors and emoluments it promised to yield. The sequel proved that his own faith was larger than that of the many, and he was content to bear a heavy burden—from which, at home, he could find relief only in part.

You are familiar with what occurred prior to the year 1858, when, after three successive failures, the "Agamemnon" and "Niagara," parting in mid-ocean, delivered their respective ends of the cable at Valentia and Trinity Bay, and with what enthusiastic applause the announcement of success was welcomed throughout our land. A grand procession, a grand dinner, splendid fireworks, and a partial conflagration of the City Hall—sparing, for a time, all below the cupola—were the distinguishing features of our Metropolitan display. The Common Council of the city and Chamber of Commerce issued medals to meritorious officers and engineers of the United States Navy who were engaged in the work, which, we then thought, was happily concluded. It was only a temporary success, and our exultation was premature and brief. Faintly the cable whispered forth "the glad tidings" of peace among men; for a few weeks gave out other signs of vitality, and then became subject to the law of death! To the doubting multitude this was a verdict of despair; to the faithful few, the promise of a new and better life. The messenger had fulfilled its mission—going before as a herald of the coming event which was to electrify the world, and hold it in wondering and perpetual awe! (Cheers.)

The general discouragement produced by the failure of 1858, the necessity for more careful preparation for another attempt, and the breaking out of civil war in the United States, put off the sailing of the next expedition to the year 1865. The great problem of the age was now to be solved; and the mammoth ship, whose mission, before, no one could interpret, was at the same time to vindicate the Providential purpose of her own creation. Bearing in her capacious hold a burden, the like of which, ship of ancient or modern times had never before carried, the "Great Eastern" sailed on her appointed voyage. Twelve hundred miles of cable were fairly laid, and then it parted. But the good ship did not forsake the lost child of science and art without divers shakes of her stretched out arm, nor without leaving her own "Buoy" as the assured pledge of her early return! And how skillfully, how faithfully was the pledge redeemed! Another year secured the final triumph. All the incidents relating to the expedition of 1866, are fresh in your recollection.

One cable being safely laid, the recovery of the other was determined on. After three weeks of diligent search and unremitting effort it was restored to the arms of the ship that bore it, and to the hands of those who had ceaselessly watched for its appearance. Darkness rested upon the surrounding waters, and sleepless eyes were turned with anxious look to the electrician who applied the magnetic test. All at once the countenances of the waiting crowd were lighted up; and in an instant the story of its rescue flashing through veins now charged with new life, reached Valentia: and behold, it was the bright morning of another day! (Loud applause.)

In every effort prior to that of 1865, the naval ships of Great Britain and of the United States were joint actors, and the partial success of 1858 was achieved under their united auspices. From that period the co-operation of our own navy was withdrawn, and the President of the United States gracefully yielded to the Sovereign of Great Britain the glory of the final triumph. It is due to candor to say that many are present who strove to have it otherwise.

In after times there will be no brighter page in English history than that which associates the laying of the Atlantic Telegraph with the reign of Queen VICTORIA. The discovery of America in 1492, gave to Queen ISABELLA of Spain "the brightest jewel of her crown," and made the name of COLUMBUS immortal! In the annals of our country, 1866 will be alike memorable as the year for uniting the two continents by an indissoluble bond; our fellow-citizen and honored guest being the prime mover and acknowledged leader in the work. (Applause.)

The British Government lost no time in rewarding the

meritorious services of all those who, being subjects of the Queen, were deemed worthy of public recognition. The honor of knighthood was at once conferred on the gallant and accomplished sailor, Capt. JAMES ANDERSON, so favorably known to our countrymen; (applause;) on Professor THOMSON, the distinguished electrician; on Messrs. GLASS and CANNING, manager and engineer, respectively, of the Telegraph Maintenance Company; on Mr. C. M. LAMPSON, a native of the United States, and steadfast supporter of the enterprise, and Mr. DANIEL GOOCH, Chairman of the Great Ship Company, "which has finally completed the design."

It was the office of Mr. CYRUS W. FIELD to organize and combine all the forces that were requisite to conduct this enterprise from its inception to the final and glorious issue. To it he devoted twelve years of his life, all his energy and all his fortune. Forty times he crossed the Atlantic Ocean for its sake; and as Captain, now Sir JAMES ANDERSON, in a recent letter says, "he has worked hard, and sacrificed the repose of his home and the repose of every one else who could bear influence on his darling scheme." (Cheers.)

I venture to say there is not an emotion known to the human soul—whether of joy or sorrow, of pleasure or pain, of disappointment following high-wrought expectation, of anxiety bordering on despair, of hope mounting to the region of sublimest faith—that during these twelve last years has not entered into the experience of our long-tried and well-proved champion. (Loud applause.)

We may fairly claim that from first to last CYRUS W. FIELD has been more closely, more consistently identified with the Atlantic Telegraph than any other living man; and his name and his fame, which the Queen of Great Britain has justly left to the care of the American Government and people, will be proudly cherished and gratefully honored. We are in daily use of the fruits of his labors; and it is meet that the men of commerce, of literature and law, of science and art—of all the professions that impart dignity and worth to our nature, should come together and give a hearty, joyous, and generous welcome to this truly chivalrous son of America.

I propose the health of our guest:

"CYRUS W. FIELD, the projector and main-spring of the Atlantic Telegraph; while the British Government justly honors those who have taken part with him in this great work of the age, *his* fame belongs to us, and will be cherished and guarded by his countrymen."

As Mr. FIELD rose to reply, he was received with long-continued applause, the whole company rising to their feet and cheering with the utmost enthusiasm. When these demonstrations had subsided, he spoke as follows:

SPEECH OF MR. FIELD.

MR. PRESIDENT: I thank you for the kind words which you have spoken; and you, gentlemen, for the manner in which you have responded to them. It is pleasant to come home after a long absence, and especially when a warm welcome meets us at the door. It is pleasant to see familiar faces and hear familiar voices; to be among old neighbors and friends, and to be assured of their regard and approbation. And now to receive such a tribute as this from the Chamber of Commerce of New-York, and from this large array of merchants and bankers and emiment citizens, is very grateful to my heart.

The scene before me awakens mingled recollections. Eight years ago the Atlantic Telegraph had won a brief success; and in this very hall we met to celebrate our victory. Alas for our hopes! How soon was our joy turned into mourning. That very day the cable departed this life. It went out like a spark in the mighty waters. So suddenly it died, that many could not believe that it ever lived. To-night we meet to rejoice in a success which I believe will be permanent. But many who were with us then are not here. Capt. HUDSON is gone to his grave. WOODHOUSE, the English engineer, who was with our own EVERETT in the "Niagara," sleeps in his native island. Others who took an early part in the work, are no more among the living. Lieut. BERRYMAN, who made the first soundings across the Atlantic, died for his country in the late war, on board his ship, off Pensacola. His companions, Lieut. STRAIN, the hero of the ill-fated Darien expedition, and Lieut. THOMAS, both are gone. So are JOHN W. BRETT, my first associate in England, SAMUEL STATHAM, Sir WILLIAM BROWN, the first Chairman of the Atlantic Telegraph Company, and many, many others. My first thought to-night is of the dead; and my only sorrow, that those who labored so faithfully with us, are not here now to share our triumph.

In the letter inviting me to accept of this Banquet, you expressed a wish to "hear from my lips the story of this great undertaking." That, Sir, would be a very long story, much beyond your patience and my strength. I should have to take you forty times across the Atlantic, and half as many to Newfoundland. Still, I will endeavor, in a brief way, to give you some faint outline of the fortunes of this enterprise.

It is nearly thirteen years since half a dozen gentlemen of this city met at my house for four successive evenings, and around a table covered with maps and charts, and plans and estimates, considered a project to extend a line of telegraph from Nova Scotia to St. John's in Newfoundland, thence to be carried across the ocean. It was a very pretty plan on paper. There was New-York, and there was St. John's, only about 1,200 miles apart. It was easy to draw a line from one point to the other—making no account of the forests and mountains, and swamps and rivers and gulfs, that lay in our way. Not one of us had ever seen the country, or had any idea of the obstacles to be overcome. We thought we could build the line in a few months. It took two years and a half. Yet we never asked for help outside our own little circle. Indeed, I fear we should not have got it if we had—for few had any faith in our scheme. Every dollar came out of our own pockets. Yet I am proud to say no man drew back. No man proved a deserter; those who came first into the work have stood by it to the end. Of those six men, four are here to-night: Mr. PETER COOPER, MOSES TAYLOR, MARSHALL O. ROBERTS, and myself. (Applause.) My brother DUDLEY is in Europe, and Mr. CHANDLER WHITE died in 1856, and his place was supplied by Mr. WILSON G. HUNT, who is also here. Mr. ROBERT W. LOWBER was our Secretary. To these gentlemen, as my first associates, it is but just that I should pay my first acknowledgments.

From this statement you perceive that in the beginning this was wholly an American enterprise. (Applause.) It was begun, and for two years and a half was carried on, solely by American capital. Our brethren across the sea did not even know what we were doing away in the forests of Newfoundland. Our little company raised and expended over a million and a quarter of dollars before an Englishman paid a single pound sterling. (Cheers.) Our only support outside was in the liberal charter and steady friendship of the Government of Newfoundland, for which we were greatly indebted to Mr. E. M. ARCHIBALD, then

Attorney-General of that colony, and now British Consul in New-York. And in preparing for an ocean cable, the first soundings across the Atlantic were made by American officers in American ships. (Applause.) Our scientific men—MORSE, HENRY, BACHE and MAURY—had taken great interest in the subject. The U. S. ship Dolphin discovered the Telegraphic Plateau as early as 1853; and the U. S. ship Arctic sounded across from Newfoundland to Ireland in 1856, a year before H. M.'s ship Cyclops, under command of Capt. DAYMAN, went over the same course. This I state, not to take aught from the just praise of England, but simply to vindicate the truth of history.

It was not till 1856—ten years ago—that the enterprise had any existence in England. In that summer I went to London, and there, with Mr. JOHN W. BRETT, Mr. (now Sir) CHARLES BRIGHT and Dr. WHITEHOUSE, organized the Atlantic Telegraph Company. Science had begun to contemplate the possibility of such an enterprise; and the great FARADAY cheered us with his lofty enthusiasm. Then for the first time was enlisted the support of English capitalists; and then the British Government began that generous course which it has continued ever since—offering us ships to complete soundings across the Atlantic, and to assist in laying the cable, and an annual subsidy for the transmission of messages. The Expedition of 1857 and the two Expeditions of 1858 were joint enterprises, in which the Niagara and the Susquehanna took part with the Agamemnon, the Leopard, the Gorgon, and the Valorous; and the officers of both navies worked with generous rivalry for the same great object. The capital—except one quarter, which, as you have said, was taken by myself—was subscribed wholly in Great Britain. The Directors were almost all English bankers and merchants, though among them was one gentleman whom we are proud to call an American, Mr. George Peabody, a name honored in two countries, since he has showered his princely benefactions upon both—who, though a resident for nearly forty years in London, where he has gained abundant wealth and honors, still clings to the land of his birth; declining the honor of a Baronetcy of the United Kingdom to remain a simple American citizen. (Loud cheers.)

With the history of the Expeditions of 1857–8 you are familiar. On the third trial we gained a brief success. The cable was laid, and for four weeks it worked, though never very brilliantly, never giving forth such rapid and distinct flashes as the cables of to-day. It spoke, though only in broken sentences. But while it lasted, no less than 400 messages were sent across the Atlantic. You all remember the enthusiasm which it excited. It was a new thing under the sun, and for a few weeks the public went wild over it. Of course, when it stopped, the reaction was very great. People grew dumb and suspicious. Some thought it was all a hoax; and many were quite sure that it never worked at all. That kind of odium we have had to endure for eight years, till now, I trust, we have at last silenced the unbelievers.

After the failure of 1858 came our darkest days. When a thing is dead, it is hard to galvanize it into life. It is more difficult to revive an old enterprise than to start a new one. The freshness and novelty are gone, and the feeling of disappointment discourages further effort.

Other causes delayed a new attempt. This country had become involved in a tremendous war; and while the nation was struggling for life, it had no time to spend in foreign enterprises.

But in England the project was still kept alive. The

Atlantic Telegraph Company kept up its organization. It had a noble body of directors, who had faith in the enterprise, and looked beyond its present low estate to ultimate success. I cannot name them all, but I must speak of our Chairman—the Right Honorable JAMES STUART WORTLEY, a gentleman who did not join us in the hour of victory, but in what seemed the hour of despair—after the failure of 1858—and who has been a steady support through all these years. The Deputy Chairman, Mr. LAMPSON, has been made a Baronet for his connection with the enterprise. Our faithful Secretary, Mr. SAWARD, too, did much to keep alive the interest of the British public.

All this time the science of submarine telegraphy was making progress. The British Government appointed a Commission to investigate the whole subject. It was composed of eminent scientific men and practical engineers—GALTON, WHEATSTONE, FAIRBAIRN, BIDDER, VARLEY, LATIMER and EDWIN CLARK—with the Secretary of the Company, Mr. SAWARD—names to be held in honor in connection with this enterprise, along with those of other English engineers, such as STEPHENSON and BRUNEL, and WHITWORTH and PENN, and LLOYD and JOSHUA FIELD, who gave time and thought and labor freely to this enterprise, refusing all compensation. This Commission sat for nearly two years, and spent many thousands of pounds in experiments. The result was a clear conviction in every mind that it *was possible* to lay a telegraph across the Atlantic. Science was also being all the while applied to practice. Submarine cables were laid in different seas—in the Mediterranean, in the Red Sea and the Persian Gulf. The latter was laid by my friend, Sir CHARLES BRIGHT, who thus rendered another service to his country, and gained a fresh title to the honor which was conferred upon him for his part in laying the first Atlantic cable.

When the scientific and engineering problems were solved, we took heart again, and began to prepare for a fresh attempt. This was in 1863. In this country—though the war was still raging—I went from city to city, holding meetings and trying to raise capital, but with poor success. Men came and listened, and said, "It was all very fine," and "hoped I would succeed," but did nothing. In one of the cities they gave me a large meeting, and passed some beautiful resolutions, and appointed a committee of "solid men" to canvass the city, but I did not get a solitary subscriber! In this city I did better, though money came by the hardest. By personal solicitations, encouraged by you, sir, and other good friends, I succeeded in raising £70,000. Since not many had faith, I must present one example to the contrary, though it was not till a year later. When almost all deemed it a hopeless scheme, one gentleman of this city came to me, and purchased stock of the Atlantic Telegraph Company to the amount of $100,000. That was Mr. LORING ANDREWS, who is here this evening to see his faith rewarded. (Applause.) But at the time I speak of, it was plain that our main hope must be in England, and I went to London. There, too, it dragged heavily. There was a profound discouragement. Many had lost before, and were not willing to throw more money into the sea. We needed £600,000, and with our utmost efforts we had raised less than half, and there the enterprise stood in a dead lock. It was plain that we must have help from some new quarter. I looked around to find a man who had broad shoulders, and could carry a heavy load, and who would be a giant in the cause. It was at this time I was introduced to a gentleman, whom

I would hold up to the American public as a specimen of a great-hearted Englishman, Mr. THOMAS BRASSEY. You may never have heard his name, but in London he is known as one of the men who have made British enterprise and British capital felt in all parts of the earth. I went to see him, though with fear and trembling. He received me kindly, but put me through such an examination as I never had before. I thought I was in the witness box. He asked every possible question, but my answers satisfied him, and he ended by saying, "It was an enterprise which ought to be carried out, and that he would be one of ten men to furnish the money to do it." This was a pledge of 60,000 pounds sterling! Encouraged by this noble offer, I looked about to find another such man, though it was almost like trying to find two WELLINGTONS. But he *was* found in Mr. JOHN PENDER, of Manchester. I went one day to his office in London, and we walked together to the House of Commons, and before we got there he said he would take an equal share with Mr. BRASSEY.

The action of these two gentlemen was a turning point in the history of our enterprise. For it led shortly after to a union of the well-known firm of GLASS, ELLIOT & Co., with the Gutta Percha Company, making of the two one grand concern, known as "THE TELEGRAPH CONSTRUCTION AND MAINTENANCE COMPANY," which included, not only Mr. BRASSEY and Mr. PENDER, but other men of great wealth, such as Mr. GEORGE ELLIOT and Mr. BARCLAY, of London, and Mr. HENRY BEWLEY, of Dublin; and which, thus reinforced with immense capital, took up the whole enterprise in its strong arms. We needed, I have said, £600,000, and with all our efforts in England and America, we had raised only £285,000. This new company now came forward, and offered to take the whole remaining £315,000—besides £100,000 of the bonds, and to make its own profits contingent on success! Mr. RICHARD A. GLASS was made Managing Director, and gave energy and vigor to all its departments, being admirably seconded by the Secretary, Mr. SHUTER. Mr. GLASS has been recently knighted for his services in carrying out the Atlantic Telegraph—an honor which he most justly deserves.

A few days after half a dozen gentlemen joined together and bought the "Great Eastern," to lay the cable; and at the head of this company was placed Mr. DANIEL GOOCH, a member of Parliament, and Chairman of the Great Western Railway, who was with us in both the expeditions which followed, and who for his services has been made a Baronet of the United Kingdom. His son, Mr. CHARLES GOOCH, a volunteer in the service, who worked faithfully on board the "Great Eastern," we are happy to welcome here to-night. (Applause.)

The good fortune which favored us in our ship favored us also in our commander. Many of you know Capt. ANDERSON—(applause)—who was for years in the CUNARD line. You may have crossed the sea with him, and you remember how kind he was; how clear-eyed and prompt in his duty, and yet always the quiet and modest gentleman. How well he did his part in two Expeditions the result has proved, and it was just that a mark of royal favor should fall on that manly head.

Thus organized, the work of making a new Atlantic Cable was begun. The core was prepared with infinite care, under the able superintendence of Mr. CHATTERTON and Mr. WILLOUGHBY SMITH; and the whole was completed in about eight months. As fast as ready, it was taken on board the "Great Eastern," and coiled in three enormous tanks; and on the 15th of July, 1865, the ship started on her memorable voyage.

I will not stop to tell the story of that Expedition. For a week all went well; we had paid out 1,200 miles of cable, and had only 600 miles farther to go, when hauling in the cable to remedy a fault, it parted and went to the bottom. That day I can never forget—how men paced the deck in despair, looking out on the broad sea that had swallowed up their hopes; and then how the brave CANNING for nine days and nights dragged the bottom of the ocean for our lost treasure, and though he grappled it three times, failed to bring it to the surface. The story of that Expedition, as written by Dr. RUSSELL, who was on board the "Great Eastern," is one of the most marvellous chapters in the whole history of modern enterprise. We returned to England defeated, yet full of resolution to begin the battle anew. Measures were at once taken to make a second cable, and fit out a new Expedition; and with that assurance I came home last autumn.

In December I went back again, when lo, all our hopes had sunk to nothing. The Attorney-General of England had given his written opinion that we had no legal right, without a special act of Parliament, (which could not be obtained under a year,) to issue the new 12 per cent. shares, on which we relied to raise our capital. This was a terrible blow. The works were at once stopped, and the money which had been paid in returned to the subscribers. Such was the state of things only ten months ago. I reached London on the 24th of December, and the next day was not a "merry Christmas" to me. But it was an inexpressible comfort to have the counsel of such men as Sir DANIEL GOOCH and Sir RICHARD A. GLASS; and to hear stout-hearted Mr. BRASSEY tell us to go ahead; and if need were, he would put down £60,000 more! It was finally concluded that the best course was *to organize a new company*, which should assume the work; and so originated the ANGLO-AMERICAN TELEGRAPH COMPANY. It was formed by ten gentlemen who met around a table in London, and put down £10,000 apiece. I hope the excellent Secretary of this Company, Mr. DEANE, who came with us across the ocean, will write its history, and tell the world what life and vigor were comprised in its Board of Directors. The great Telegraph Construction and Maintenance Company—undaunted by the failure of last year—answered us with a subscription of £100,000. Soon after, the books were opened to the public, through the eminent banking house of J. S. MORGAN & Co., and in fourteen days we had raised the whole £600,000. (Loud applause.) Then the work began again, and went on with speed. Never was greater energy infused into any enterprise. It was only the first day of March that the new company was formed, and was registered as a company the next day; and yet such was the vigor and despatch, that in five months from that day the cable had been manufactured, shipped on the "Great Eastern," stretched across the Atlantic, and was sending messages, literally swift as lightning, from continent to continent. (Prolonged cheers.)

Yet this was not "a lucky hit"—a fine run across the ocean in calm weather. It was the worst weather I ever knew at that season of the year. In the despatch which appeared in the New-York papers you may have read, "The weather has been most pleasant." I wrote it "*un*-pleasant." We had fogs and storms almost the whole way. Our success was the result of the highest science combined with practical experience. Every thing was perfectly organized to the minutest detail. We had on board an admirable staff of officers, such men as HALPIN and BECKWITH; and engineers long used to this business, such as CANNING, and CLIFFORD, and TEMPLE, the first of whom has been knighted for his part in this great achievement; and electricians, such as Professor THOMSON, of Glasgow, and WILLOUGHBY SMITH, and LAWS; while Mr. C. F. VARLEY, our companion of the year before, who stands among the first in knowledge and practical skill, remained with Sir RICHARD GLASS at Valentia, to keep watch at that end of the line; and Mr. LATIMER CLARK, who was to test the cable when done. Of these gentlemen, Professor THOMSON, as one of the earliest and most eminent electricians of England, has received the same mark of distinction. England honors herself when she thus pays honor to science; and it is fit that the government which honored chemistry in Sir HUMPHREY DAVY, should honor electrical science in Sir WILLIAM THOMSON. (Applause.)

But our work was not over. After landing the cable safely at Newfoundland, we had another task—to return to mid-ocean and recover that lost in the expedition of last year. This achievement has perhaps excited more surprise than the other. Many even now "don't understand it," and every day I am asked, "how it was done?" Well, it does seem rather difficult to fish for a jewel at the bottom of the ocean two and a half miles deep. But it is not so *very* difficult—when you know how. You may be sure we did not go a-fishing at random, nor was our success mere "luck." It was the triumph of the highest nautical and engineering skill. We had four ships, and on board of them some of the best seamen in England, men who knew the ocean as a hunter knows every trail in the forest. There was Capt. MORIARTY, who was in the "Agamemnon" in 1857–8. He was in the "Great Eastern" last year, and saw the cable when it broke; and he and Capt. ANDERSON at once took their observations so exact that they could go right to the spot. After finding it, they marked the line of the cable by a row of buoys; for fogs would come down, and shut out sun and stars, so that no man could take an observation. These buoys were anchored a few miles apart. They were numbered, and each had a flag-staff on it, so that it could be seen by day; and a lantern by night. Thus having taken our bearings, we stood off three or four miles, so as to come broadside on, and then casting over the grapnel, drifted slowly down upon it, dragging the bottom of the ocean as we went. At first it was a little awkward to fish in such deep water, but our men got used to it, and soon could cast a grapnel almost as straight as an old whaler throws a harpoon. Our fishing line was of formidable size. It was made of rope, twisted with wires of steel, so as to bear a strain of thirty tons. It took about two hours for the grapnel to reach bottom, but we could tell when it struck. I often went to the bow and sat on the rope, and could feel by the quiver that the grapnel was dragging on the bottom two miles under us. (Applause.) But it was a very slow business. We had storms and calms, and fogs and squalls. Still we worked on day after day. Once, on the 17th of August, we got the cable up and had it in full sight for five minutes, a long, slimy monster, fresh from the ooze of the ocean's bed; but our men began to cheer so wildly, that it seemed to be frightened, and suddenly broke away and went down into the sea. This accident kept us at work two weeks longer, but finally, on the last night of August, we caught it. We had cast the grapnel thirty times. It was a little before midnight on Friday night that we hooked the cable, and it was a little after midnight, Sunday morning, when we got it on board. (Cheers.) What was the anxiety of those twenty-six hours! The strain on every man's life was like the strain on the cable itself. When finally it appeared, it was midnight; the lights of the ship, and in the boats around our bows, as they flashed in the faces of the men, showed them eagerly watching for the cable to appear on the water. At length it was brought to the surface. All who were allowed to approach crowded forward to see it. Yet not a word was spoken; only the voices of the officers in command were heard giving orders. All felt as if life and death hung on the issue. It was only when it was brought over the bow and on to the deck that men dared to breathe. Even then they hardly believed their eyes. Some crept toward it to feel of it, to be sure it was there. Then we carried it along to the electricians' room, to see if our long sought treasure was alive or dead. A few minutes of suspense, and a flash told of the lightning current again set free. Then did the feeling long pent up burst forth. Some turned away their heads and wept. Others broke into cheers, and the cry ran from man to man, and was heard down in the engine rooms, deck below deck, and from the boats on the water, and the other ships, while rockets lighted up the darkness of the sea. Then with thankful hearts we turned our faces again to the west. But soon the wind rose, and for thirty-six hours we were exposed to all the dangers of a storm on the Atlantic. Yet, in the very height and fury of the gale, as I sat in the electricians' room, a flash of light came up from the deep, which having crossed to Ireland, came back to me in mid-ocean, telling that those so dear to me, whom I had left on the banks of the Hudson, were well, and following us with their wishes and their prayers. (Applause.) This was like a whisper of God from the sea, bidding me keep heart and hope. The "Great Eastern" bore herself proudly through the storm, as if she knew that the vital chord, which was to join two hemispheres, hung at her stern; and so, on Saturday, the 7th of September, we brought our second cable safely to the shore. (Renewed applause.)

But the "Great Eastern" did not make her voyage alone. Three other ships attended her across the ocean—the "Albany," the "Medway" and the "Terrible"—the officers of all of which exerted themselves to the utmost. The Queen of England has shown her appreciation of the services of some of those more prominent in the expedition, but if it had been possible to do justice to all, honors would have been bestowed upon many others. If this cannot be, at least let their names live in the history of this enterprise, with which they will be forever associated.

When I think of them all—not only of those on the "Great Eastern," but of Capt. COMMERILL, of the "Terrible," and his first officer, Mr. CURTIS, (who with their ship came with us not only to Heart's Content, but afterwards to the Gulf of St. Lawrence, to help in laying the new cable,) and of the officers of the other ships, my heart is full. Better men never trod a deck. If I do not name them all, it is because they are too many, their ranks are too full of glory. Even the sailors caught the enthusiasm of the enterprise, and were eager to share in the honor of the achievement. Brave, stalwart men they were—at home on the ocean and in the storm—of that sort that have carried the flag of England around the globe. (Cheers.) I see them now as they dragged the shore end up the beach at Heart's Content, hugging it in their brawny arms as if it were a shipwrecked child whom they had rescued from the dangers of the sea. God bless them all! (Applause.)

Such, gentlemen, in brief, is the story of the Telegraph which you have wished to hear. It has been a long, hard struggle—nearly thirteen years of anxious watching and ceaseless toil. Often my heart has been ready to sink. Many times, when wandering in the forests of Newfoundland, in the pelting rain, or on the deck of ships, on dark, stormy nights—alone, far from home—I have almost accused myself of madness and folly to sacrifice the peace of my family, and all the hopes of life, for what might prove after all but a dream. I have seen my companions one and another falling by my side, and feared that I too might not live to see the end. And yet one hope has led me on, and I have prayed that I might not taste of death till this work was accomplished. That prayer is answered: and now, beyond all acknowledgments to men, is the feeling of gratitude to Almighty God. (Deep sensation and applause.)

Having thus accomplished our work of building an Ocean Telegraph, we desire to make it useful to the public. To this end it must be kept in perfect order, and all lines connected with it. The very idea of an electric telegraph is, an instrument to send messages *instantaneously.* When a despatch is sent from New-York to London, there must be no uncertainty about its reaching its destination—and that promptly. This we aim to secure. Our two cables do their part well. There are no way stations between Ireland and Newfoundland, where messages have to be repeated, and the lightning never lingers *more than a second* in the bottom of the sea. To those who feared that they might be used up or wear out, I would say, for their relief, that the old cable works a little better than the new one, but that is because it has been down longer, as time improves the quality of gutta percha. But the new one is constantly growing better. To show how delicate are these wonderful chords, it is enough to state that they can be worked with the smallest battery power. When the first cable was laid in 1858, electricians thought that to send a current two thousand miles, it must be almost like a stroke of lightning. But God was not in the earthquake, but in the still, small voice. The other day Mr. LATIMER CLARK telegraphed from Ireland across the Ocean and back again, with a battery formed in a lady's thimble! (Applause.) And now Mr. COLLETT writes me from Heart's Content: "I have just sent my compliments to Dr. GOULD, of Cambridge, who is at Valentia, with a battery composed of a gun cap, with a strip of zinc, excited by a drop of water, the simple bulk of a tear!" (Renewed applause.) A telegraph that will do that we think nearly perfect. It has never failed for an hour or a minute. Yet there have been delays in receiving messages from Europe, but these have all been *on the land lines* or in the Gulf of St. Lawrence, and not on the sea cables. It was very painful to me, when we landed at Heart's Content, to find any interruption here, that a message which came in a flash across the Atlantic, should be delayed twenty-four hours in crossing eighty miles of water. But it was not my fault. My associates in the Newfoundland Company will bear me witness, that I entreated them a year ago to repair the cable in the Gulf of St. Lawrence, and to put our land lines in perfect order. But they thought it more prudent to await the result of the late Expedition before making further large outlays. We have therefore had to work hard to restore our lines. But in two weeks our cable across the Gulf of St. Lawrence was taken up and repaired. It was found to have been broken by an anchor in shallow water, and, when spliced out, proved as perfect as when laid down ten years ago. Since then a new one has been laid, so that we have there two excellent cables.

On land the task was more slow. You must remember that Newfoundland is a large country; our line across it is 400 miles long, and runs through a wilderness. In Cape Breton we have another of 140 miles. These lines were built twelve years ago, and we have waited so long for an ocean telegraph that they have become old and rusty. On such long lines, unless closely watched, there must be sometimes a break. A few weeks ago a storm swept over the island, the most terrific that had been known for twenty years, which strewed the coast with shipwrecks. This blew down the line in many places, and caused an interruption of several days. But it was quickly repaired, and we are trying to guard against such accidents again. For three months we have had an army of men at work, under our faithful and indefatigable Superintendent, Mr. A. M. Mackay, rebuilding the line, and now they report it nearly complete. On this we must rely for the next few months. But all winter long these men will be making their axes heard in the forests of Newfoundland, cutting thousands of poles, and as soon as the spring opens will build an entirely new line along the same route. With this double line complete, with frequent station houses, and faithful sentinels to watch it, we feel pretty secure. At Port Hood, in Nova Scotia, we connect with the Western Union Telegraph Company, which has engaged to keep as many lines as may be necessary for European business. This we think will guard against failures hereafter. But to make assurance doubly sure, we shall in the spring build still another line by a separate route, crossing over from Heart's Content to Placentia, which is only about a hundred miles, along a good road, where it can easily be kept in order. From Placentia a submarine cable will be laid across to the French island of St. Pierre, and thence to Sydney, in Cape Breton, where again we strike a coach road, and can maintain our lines without difficulty. Thus we shall have *three distinct lines*, with which it is hardly possible that there can be any delay. A message from London to New-York passes over four lines: from London to Valentia; from

Valentia to Heart's Content; from there to Port Hood, and from Port Hood to New-York. It always takes a little time for an operator to read a message, and prepare to send it. For this allow five minutes at each station—that is enough, and I shall not be content till we have messages regularly from London in twenty minutes. One hour is ample (allowing ten minutes each side for a boy to carry a despatch) for a message to go from Wall-street to the Royal Exchange and to get an answer back again. This is what we aim to do. If for a few months there should be occasional delays, we ask only a little patience, remembering that our machinery is new, and it takes time to get it well-oiled and running at full speed. But after that I trust we shall be able to satisfy all the demands of the public.

A word about the tariff. Complaint has been made that it was so high, as to be very oppressive. I beg all to remember, that it is only three months and a half since the cable was laid. It was laid at a great cost and a great risk. Different companies had sunk in their attempts twelve millions of dollars. It was still an experiment, of which the result was doubtful. This, too, might prove another costly failure. Even if successful, we did not know how long it would work. Evil prophets in both countries predicted that it would not last a month. If it did, we were not sure of having more than one cable; nor how much work that one could do. Now these doubts are resolved. We have, not only one cable, but two, both in working order; and we find, instead of five words a minute, we can send fifteen. Now we are free to reduce the tariff. Accordingly it has been cut down one-half, and I hope in a few months we can bring it down to one-quarter. I am in favor of reducing it to the lowest point at which we can do the business, keeping the lines working day and night. And then—if the work grows upon us so enormously that we cannot do it—why we must go to work and lay more cables. (Applause.)

Those who conduct a public enterprise ought not to object to any fair criticism of the public or the press. But complaints are sometimes made without reflection, as when fault is found with the cable, because the news from Europe may be scanty or unimportant, as if we had any more to do with what passes over the line, than the Post Office Department with the contents of letters that go through the mail. We are common carriers, and send whatever comes; and if our brethren of the Press keep capable men in the capitals of Europe, who will furnish only news which *is* important, we will see that it is delivered here every morning.

Of the results of this enterprise—commercially and politically—it is for others to speak. To one effect only do I refer as the wish of my heart—that, as it brings us into closer relations with England, it may produce a better understanding between the two countries. Let who will speak against England—words of censure must come from other lips than mine. I have received too much kindness from Englishmen to join in this language. I have eaten of their bread and drank of their cup, and I have received from them, in the darkest hours of this enterprise, words of cheer which I shall never forget; and if any words of mine can tend to peace and good will, they shall not be wanting. I beg my countrymen to remember the ties of kindred. Blood is thicker than water. America with all her greatness has come out of the loins of England; and though there have been sometimes family quarrels—bitter as family quarrels are apt to be—still in our hearts there is a yearning for the old home, the land of our fathers; and he is an enemy of his country and of the human race, who would stir up strife between two nations that are one in race, in language and in religion. (Applause.) I close with this sentiment: ENGLAND AND AMERICA—CLASPING HANDS ACROSS THE SEA, MAY THIS FIRM GRASP BE A PLEDGE OF FRIENDSHIP TO ALL GENERATIONS! (Enthusiastic applause—the audience rising and giving three cheers.)

TELEGRAPHIC DESPATCHES.

The President said: Ladies and Gentlemen, before announcing the next toast, the Chair feels under the necessity of discharging a little of the electricity with which Gen. LEFFERTS has been steadily plying the Chair since we came into this room.

STATE DEPARTMENT, WASHINGTON, *Nov.* 15, 1866.

A. A. LOW, Esq., *Metropolitan Hotel, New-York:*

CYRUS W. FIELD: The first, the most constant and the most energetic friend in the United States of the latest accomplished great enterprise in the advance of universal civilization.

WM. H. SEWARD.

(Long and continued cheering.)

From the Governor of Newfoundland.

ST. JOHN'S, NEWFOUNDLAND, *Nov.* 15*th*.

CYRUS W. FIELD, Esq.:

I greatly regret that I am unable to accept the invitation to be present at the banquet to-night. It would have given me much pleasure to meet the Directors of the New-York, Newfoundland and London Telegraph Company, who were the pioneers in the line of communication which now unites Europe and America; and I should have been proud on this occasion to represent the Colony of Newfoundland, which so liberally acted in the first steps toward the accomplishment of the great work now successfully completed, which must strengthen the ties which attach our two nations.

A. MUSGRAVE.

From Sir James Anderson, Captain of the Great Eastern.

LONDON, ENGLAND, *Nov.* 15*th.*

A. A. Low, Esq., *President Chamber of Commerce, New-York:*

Will you tell Mr. FIELD, at your Banquet, that I am with him in hearty friendship, and hope his countrymen will give due recognition to his unequalled efforts to establish the telegraphic cord between the two countries.

JAMES ANDERSON.

(Loud applause.)

From Lord Monck, Governor-General of Canada.

QUEBEC, C. E., *Nov.* 15*th.*

To the Committee of the Chamber of Commerce of City of New-York:

GENTLEMEN:

Your invitation only reached me this day. Had I been able to avail myself of it, I should have felt the greatest pleasure in joining with you to do honor to your eminent countryman, who has taken so distinguished a part in achieving the triumphant success which you this evening celebrate.

MONCK.

WASHINGTON, D. C., *Nov.* 15*th.*

A. A. Low, Esq., *New-York:*

Regretting my inability to be present with yourself and others to exchange congratulations with our friend FIELD on the happy result of his efforts to unite the Old World with the New, my best wishes are with you and all who participated in the enterprise. Should the union thus formed be broken, may it have a speedy reconstruction.

GIDEON WELLES, *Secretary of the Navy.*

WASHINGTON, *Thursday, Nov.* 15*th.*

A. A. Low, Esq., *Metropolitan Hotel, New-York:*

My congratulations to your interesting gathering, and to the worthy recipient of its honors, CYRUS W. FIELD, on the completion of the most wonderful enterprise of modern times. Please accept as a sentiment from me, "The Unity of America and Europe, in Peace, Progress and Prosperity, strengthened in both Hemispheres by the Atlantic Telegraph and its Railway adjuncts."

O. H. BROWNING, *Secretary of the Interior.*

WASHINGTON, *Thursday, Nov.* 15*th.*

A. A. LOW,

Chairman Committee of Arrangements, Metropolitan Hotel, New-York:

I regret that other engagements prevent my joining in your welcome to CYRUS W. FIELD, the greatest funambulist the world ever saw, who has walked into immortal renown over a rope three thousand miles long. The great and loyal West, standing midway between the antipodes, stretches her hands to greet the man who has united them in the bonds of everlasting brotherhood.

JOHN A. LOGAN.

NEW-GLASGOW, N. S., *Nov.* 15*th,* 1866.

CYRUS W. FIELD:

Nova Scotia rejoices most sincerely, and begs to offer you her share of congratulations upon the triumphant success which has, by the blessing of Providence, finally crowned your noble energy and perseverance in uniting Europe and America by the bonds of the submarine telegraph.

JESSE HOYT.

The following was sent to the chair:

November 15*th.*

CYRUS W. FIELD, Esq.:

I received to-day over the cable a despatch from REUTER, announcing that NAPOLEON had ordered a conscription of sailors throughout the French maritime provinces to man the vessels to bring home the French troops from Mexico. It seems to be a favorable opportunity to announce such news, as fully confirming NAPOLEON'S intention to withdraw from Mexico immediately.

J. McLEAN, *Reuter's Agent.*

(The reading of the above was received with an outburst of the most enthusiastic cheers, all present rising to their feet and waving handkerchiefs.)

THE CHAIRMAN: There are other telegrams; but I will now proceed with the work of the evening, and I deem it fortunate that we have with us, this evening, a gentleman whose name is intimately associated with the interests of the country, and sheds a light upon the present as well as upon the past—a man whose eloquence is sure to be heard with patriotic ring wherever the American heart is stirred to noble measures. I am permitted to call upon the President of the Union League Club of New-York, JOHN JAY, Esq., to respond to the toast which you have heard:

"*England and America*—clasping hands across the sea—may their grasp be a pledge of friendship to all generations."

REMARKS OF THE HON. JOHN JAY.

Mr. PRESIDENT: I am well aware of the delicacy of the task which you impose, when, on behalf of the Chamber of Commerce of New-York, you honor me with a request to respond to the toast—England and America clasping hands across the sea—which has been so cordially received by this assemblage. Certainly that toast could have been offered by no one more appropriately than by your distinguished guest, who, in the achievement which we have met to celebrate, represented to a great extent both countries, and conferred a signal benefit on both, and whose interesting story of the cable, completing your own graphic sketch of the undertaking, we have listened to with pleasure and with pride.

A short time since it would have been easy, in acknowledging a sentiment like this, to arouse the hearty enthusiasm of such a company as is here assembled, representing the culture, the wealth, the commercial greatness, the social power of the national metropolis, by invocations, however trite and tame, to the ties of ancestry and kindred that still linked our young Republic with the mother land; a common language, literature and law; the same Bible, the same *habeas corpus*, the same trial by jury, and a common property in the English historians from BEDE to BANCROFT, and in the English poets, from SPENCER and CHAUCER to LONGFELLOW and BRYANT. But now, a response simply of that sort, without a word of reference to the events of the past five years, which in their stern distinctness are present to our thoughts, would be felt by all, whether Americans or Englishmen, to be unmanly and unreal. Brief as is the period that has elapsed, the America of to-day differs from the America that hailed the success of the cable in 1858 with the joyous festivities to which you have alluded, as the thoughtful man who has fought the great battle of life, and conquered through trial and disappointment, differs from the thoughtless and inexperienced youth still rejoicing in his confidence and credulity. With the courtesy, therefore, and cordial feeling appropriate to an occasion like the present, may be fitly blended a little of that friendly frankness which Englishmen are accustomed to use toward each other, and which none know better than Englishmen how to appreciate, when honestly exhibited toward themselves.

The members of the Chamber of Commerce who have honored the toast to England and America, are interested not simply as are the American people, on national grounds, but in part more directly, in the still pending questions that, having taxed the diplomacy of Mr. ADAMS and Earl RUSSELL, await the action of the DERBY Government. Around us are gentlemen whose names are known on both sides of the Atlantic by the largeness of their international charities, and by their scrupulous adherence to the duties of international neutrality, with which your own name, Sir, is so conspicuously and honorably associated; and when these gentlemen, who have certainly no pressing reasons to regard England with special affection, exchange a personal for a national standpoint, and with the foresight of true statesmanship, looking beyond the mistakes of the past and the complications of the present, and calmly regarding the distant future, the interests of posterity and the mission of the two countries in advancing together the civilization and freedom of the world;

when these gentlemen, with such views, hail the ocean cable, whose success is chiefly due to our friend and guest, as a new and lasting link between England and America; when they join, as they have done, in the hope, if not the prayer, expressed in this toast, that it may be a pledge of friendship to all generations, I think, Sir, that this toast has a significance which no similar sentiment, on a similar occasion, ever had or could have had before. (Applause.) It is justified by the cable telegram this very morning, advising us of the inclination of the English Government and the English people to amicably settle and adjust all the American claims, including that under the Alabama, whenever such action is demanded by the American Cabinet; and your cordial reception of this toast will in turn advise England that we are inclined to accept that announcement, strengthened as it is by the changed opinion of her press and the more courteous tone of her statesmen, as an indication that she is ready to do speedy and ample justice, so far as justice may still be done, and as an assurance that the errors of the past will never be repeated.

Your response to Mr. FIELD's sentiment shows that you do not confound the narrow prejudices of a class, nor the temporary policy of a Cabinet, with the broad instincts and sympathies of a nation. That we remember cordially the hundreds of thousands of Englishmen against whom we have no complaint, in all ranks and circles of English life, from the palace of the Queen to the stately homes of ARGYLE and of STANLEY; from our fast friends, the great champion of the people, JOHN BRIGHT, (loud cheers,) and the late Regius Professor at Oxford, that representative of the classic scholarship of England, GOLDWIN SMITH, (renewed applause,) down to the humblest of the English operatives, who, with the "simple faith" that TENNYSON says is more than "Norman blood," in the very face of starvation, adhered firmly to the cause of the American Republic and of American freedom. It shows also that we have not forgotten, and are not ready to forget, the deep-felt spontaneous and universal burst of sympathy, that came to us after the death of LINCOLN, which Mr. DISRAELI said was one of those rare instances where the sympathy of a nation approaches those tenderer feelings which are generally supposed to be peculiar to the individual and the privilege of private life.

Lastly, Sir, does it not indicate, in some degree at least, the high and honorable tone of the foreign policy which the Chamber of Commerce, and the influential class which it largely represents, deem fitting for our country at this moment of her rising greatness, when the Union is about to be restored in all its national completeness, upon the basis of equal right and equal justice between State and State and man and man? (Applause.) Europe is being advised by her political writers to fear our military and naval power, to anticipate the coming day when we shall number our hundred millions; and she is warned to combine in advance to resist an American invasion. These gentlemen evidently believe that our future illustrations of the principle of non-intervention, of which we have demanded so strict an observance towards ourselves, will add new force to the definition of TALLEYRAND, who, while minister to England, on being asked by a lady the meaning of non-intervention, replied, "Madame, non-intervention is a diplomatic and enigmatical word, which means nearly the same thing as intervention." (Laughter.) The tone of this assemblage may help to disabuse Europe of the impression that we shall follow European example in meddling with the affairs of other States, whether great or small; may teach them that, however gigantic our military or naval strength, we propose rather to advance the happiness of the world by the peaceful influence of our principles, and the moral force of our example; that we rejoice in the ocean cable, not simply on grounds of commerce and convenience, but as enabling the voice of America to be instantaneously heard in Europe; and that our foreign policy is one of peace, harmony and justice, not only with England but with the world. (Loud applause.)

The next regular toast on the list was then read:

The New-York, Newfoundland and London Telegraph—Passing through the wilderness to the sea—forerunner of the Transatlantic line.

Mr. Low: It is said of good men that "their works do follow them." This toast will be responded to by our venerable friend, the President of the New-York, Newfoundland and London Telegraph Company, whose goods works go before him, and are ever present all around him. (Applause.) I have the pleasure of presenting Mr. Peter Cooper.

Address of Peter Cooper, Esq.

Mr. President and Gentlemen: In the toast you have drank in honor of the New-York, Newfoundland and London Telegraph Company, you have said, Mr. President, that our company has, by passing a line of telegraph through the wilderness to the sea, become the forerunner of the Atlantic line.

You might have said, Mr. President, with great propriety, that our company has not only been the forerunner, but was, in fact, the originator of the Trans-Atlantic line.

This will appear from the fact that our charter declares

that, "*Whereas* it is deemed advisable to establish telegraphic communication between the United States and Europe, by the way of Newfoundland: *Be it therefore enacted*, That Peter Cooper, Moses Taylor, Cyrus W. Field and Marshall O. Roberts, and others, be incorporated for that purpose." In compliance with that charter we have laid a cable through that great arm of the sea, the Gulf of St. Lawrence. The effort to lay this cable was attended with both difficulty and danger. We not only lost our cable by the unfortunate management of our captain, but came near losing the vessel, with all lives on board.

We then had to order another cable, which was finally laid, and worked successfully for nine years, when that cable was broken by the anchor of a vessel.

After several unsuccessful efforts to restore this cable, we at last succeeded, and it is now working more perfectly than it did when it was first put down. During our efforts to restore this cable, and fearing that we might not be successful, we ordered a third cable to be laid by one of the same vessels that attended the "Great Eastern" in the laying of the Atlantic cable. (Applause.)

We have now two perfect cables working across the Gulf of St. Lawrence, and two cables across the Straits of Northumberland, besides cables across several smaller streams. We shall soon have two complete lines through tne wilderness in Newfoundland and Nova Scotia.

We are now making arrangements for putting down another ocean line of some three hundred miles in length. This line, when completed, will connect Newfoundland with the French island of St. Pierre, and Nova Scotia, and will give us a water line, avoiding a great part of the Indian country through which we have been compelled to pass.

By these several lines, forming, as they do, a part of the great Atlantic line, we have now the satisfaction to believe that our communication with the European world will soon be as perfect as human ingenuity can make it.

As you have just heard from Mr. FIELD, the Atlantic line is now so perfect that a battery of a single drop of water has been sufficient to send a message across the ocean. (Cheers.)

Nearly thirteen years of unceasing toil, labor and expense have been required to complete a work that now commands the admiration and wonder of the world.

Our honored guest has shown how entirely inadequate human language is to draw to the life a picture of such scenes as those through which he and our company have been compelled to pass.

Nothing short of the energy, skill and courage of CYRUS W. FIELD could have inspired his associates with courage to go on through thirteen long and anxious years, constantly expending money, and receiving nothing in return.

Thanks to a kind Providence, we have at last been led by the light of science to a result that is now destined to prove a blessing to the world. This triumph of science and labor will be better understood, when the amount of business offered shall enable the companies to reduce the price to the lowest point that will pay a suitable compensation for the vast amount that has been expended to accomplish the work. It only needs one moment's reflection on the boundless field out of which business will finally flow to this line, to form some idea of its real value to the world in the future.

For one, Mr. President, I rejoice in every application of science to any and all of the useful purposes of life.

I rejoice in the belief that science will yet develope and make plain the laws and purposes of Deity.

I trust that the light of science, which is the light of God, will finally dispel the clouds of ignorance which prevent mankind from seeing that the right and wise use of everything is a virtue and a good, whilst the wrong and excessive use of anything is an evil and a mistake, which it is the interest of all men everywhere to avoid.

I rejoice in the hope that the work in which our friend and guest has borne so noble a part, will yet be the means of sending through the world with lightning speed a better knowledge of the fact that God has given to man the world and all that in it is, and only requires that we shall keep, subdue and hold dominion, by exercising a right or righteous government over it. (Applause.)

Gentlemen, I will give you a sentiment. I give you, gentlemen: "Our glorious Union of States, bound to a common humanity by an electric chain. May it tend to establish justice as the only possible way to promote a world's welfare."

THE CHAIRMAN: The sixth regular toast is—

The Western Union Telegraph and the Russian Extension—The American and Asiatic links of the chain encircling the globe.

The gentleman who will speak to the toast is too well known to require any announcement other than of his own name. The Chair will call upon Rev. Dr. BELLOWS. (Applause.)

ADDRESS OF REV. HENRY W. BELLOWS, D. D.

MR. PRESIDENT AND GENTLEMEN: Brevity, I believe, is the soul of wit, and especially on telegraphic occasions; and therefore I shall endeavor to condense in very few words what I think, with sufficient time, might be properly expanded over very large space.

Our thoughts and our eyes have thus far very naturally been directed Eastward, across that stormy Atlantic which has had its iron bridle slipped under it so adroitly by our distinguished guest and his co-workers. It seems to be time to face about and look in the other direction, westward and across the broad and mild-tempered Pacific. For the United States, looked at on MERCATOR's projection, seems to hold the central position on the globe, just midway between the great oceans, fronting at either face on Europe and Asia; but with nearly three-quarters of the one thousand millions of the earth's population standing on the other side of the Pacific, and inviting the trade and commerce of an enterprising and new country into the greatest market of the world. Already a sure instinct has led the vigorous men of the Empire State to throw out the cords of their tents towards the Pacific, and it is a source of pride to know that the capital and the brains invested in that immense enterprise, The Western Union Telegraph Company, with its paid-in capital of $20,000,000, came chiefly, not from the great commercial and financial mart in which we are assembled, but from an inland town of this State, Rochester, a town which, knowing the disadvantages of isolation, projected a plan for bringing the whole American territory into close contact, and shrinking this continent into a manageable shape and a convenient bulk for Liberty and Union to handle and hold on to. (Cheers.)

Who can tell what this country already owes for its integrity to the Western Union Telegraph Company? Did it not keep the heart of our whole Pacific brotherhood, separated by deserts and mountains, or otherwise approachable only by a voyage of five thousand miles, beating towards us with all the regularity of two chronometers, timed to each other, through our great war?

(Cheers.) No one has a better right than I to speak of the value of that telegraph wire. Part of the time, all through the war, I was using it, almost regardless of expense, to send tidings and thanks and urgent demands to the noble patriots in California, Oregon and Nevada; and part of the time I was listening in California to its daily click as it told us in San Francisco how the terrible battles of the Wilderness were advancing, and how GRANT was "fighting it out on that line," although it took him not only all that summer, but pretty much all the next. (Applause.)

But it is not what the Western Union Telegraph has done on this continent, vast and priceless as its benefits are, that engages our chief interest to-night. There is nothing *National* or purely *American* in this occasion. Telegraph companies are now not content with continental proportions; their thoughts are cosmical; they, like those universal philanthropists and Christians who say "our Field is the world," contemplate the physical geography of the whole globe, as they proceed to throw their thinking and speaking wires about it, and touching it here and there with their electric fingers, communicate a common consciousness to its complete surface.

And so, when the Western Union Telegraph Company saw the brave capitalist and telegraphist of America seeking to bind Europe to American commerce, and saw him, like a spent swimmer, sinking again and again with his prize, until they doubted whether he would ever come to the surface again, they devised the Overland Telegraph to Europe through Asia; certainly, one of the boldest and most magnificent enterprises ever conceived by man. "There be land-rats, and there be water-rats;" there be under-sea telegraphers and overland telegraphers, and certainly, for polar regions, telegraphs *on poles* have a natural claim to superiority over telegraphs under water. At any rate, the Russian Extension of the Western Union Telegraph, which we owe to the vigorous enterprise and personal address of Mr. Perry McDonough Collins—who carries victory in his very name—aided by the confidence of American capitalists, has chosen the land, and not water, for its theatre of glory. And what an inconceivable stretch of territory it does present to our imagination! Why, sir, it appalls one's powers of syllabication and utterance to merely mention the countries, towns and cities through which this line of telegraph already passes; all the gutturals, sneezes and labials; all the endless vowelless cataract of consonants, in Indian, Tchutchi, Orkotch and Irkoutch; with all the itskys and bitskys, chows and changs, of Russian and Polish, of Mongolian and Chinese and Japanese languages, will not serve to express the confusion of tongues, worse than the original Babel, which the mere crowding or stringing so many nations on one string, like dried-apples in a New-England farm-house, produces, at least, in the imagination. (Applause.)

But to contemplate seriously the wonderful prospective effect of this commerce with Asia on our national—nay, on what is far beyond that—our *common human prospects*, is most kindling to the larger feelings of that cosmopolite soul, which the Maker hid in the orb-like brain of man. I might spend the remainder of this whole evening in reminding you of the inestimable value of the trade which is opened among its seven hundred and fifty millions by this network of telegraphs, with which the Russian Extension is connecting you, even as a handle is connected with the net with which you fish. I might remind you that your sables and ermines, your beavers and foxes and wolverines, in short, that all the precious furs that serve your comfort and elegance, come from British and Russian America; that your whaling fleets find stations in the immediate neighborhood of this line; that your teas, your silks, your spices, your ginger and your dyes are collected in China, India and Japan; and that millions are there waiting to exchange the silver hoard of ages with the products of your ingenuity. I might, perhaps, touch your fancy by giving you a short ride in Kamscatka, behind a team of dogs, or, better, a sledge-ride in Siberia, behind a well-trained reindeer, or lift you on a camel or an elephant pacing beside the line of your telegraph track in some portion of its way. I could carry you by the remains of temples as old as Marco Polo's descriptions, and show you the ruins of Genghis Khan's invasion. I could lead you to the fairs of Novogorod, or introduce you to the eight-year old boy who is waiting for his imperial crown in China, if Russia don't run away with it before he grows up, or step across and call on the Tycoon, or even, what would be far more agreeable, chat an hour with friend Burlingame at Pekin.

But all these interesting considerations—inflaming to fancy, fragrant with odors and gums and spices, bright with gems and purple colors, and wrapped in polychromatic shawls—bringing, too, the regions of the Chinese Wall, the Arabian Nights, and even the holy deserts of Sinai and the sacred places where our religion began, to our thoughts; all these considerations yield in dignity and importance to the thought that Asia, the still most populous part of the world, is coming again into the circle of civilization, within the reach of modern ideas, near to Christian sympathies and feelings, and within the hand-grasp of Europe and America. (Cheers.)

Nor is it only what is to be *given* her that we have to think of, even in the mission of ideas. Asia is still alive in the thoughts she stands for! Religion! Revelation had her fountain-head there, humanly speaking, because the East is, by constitution, temperament and providential fitness, more eminently meditative and devout. The masculine *will*, the active, and not the passive soul, is developed in Europe, and still more in America. But it is the female element that bears the germs of all things. Asia has thoughts, feelings, experiences, that need to be added to cosmopolitan civilization, and which might even suggest valuable lessons to faith and piety. The sense of fate, which is only an over-sense of God, is the native fruit of Oriental lands.

I believe in the unity of the race, and in the absolute necessity of bringing all the quarters of the globe into concert before a full harmony will be struck. (Applause.)

I might, I ought to say a word of the union between America and Russia which this extension typifies and cements..... The rapid and noble efforts to reach the Amoor, which that gigantic empire of the Czars has made, shows the largeness of the spirit which animates that young Colossus, modern Russia. It has reached the Straits and strides them, but it is only to extend a hand of perfect sympathy to her continental peer, the young nation that, like herself, is still in early boyhood, and has the enterprise of unexpended spirits and unfettered room. The Russian and the American eagles fly together, and without temptation to quarrel. In our great extremity, cordial expressions of sympathy came, not from old allies, or our cousins and relations, but from the nation with which we had least political affinity and least commercial intercourse, and least lingual or personal connection. We may well rejoice that the two powers of greatest territorial expansion, and perhaps greatest military force, are now warm friends, and closing up the distance between them by an increasing knowledge of each other, a growing commerce in the Amoor and the Baltic, and by this wondrous telegraphic wire. (Applause.)

I close with giving you a toast, which has a feeble pun in it that may be excused:

Russia and America: May they always meet in a Pacific sea, and never find themselves in Straits so narrow that they do not remember their mutual *Behrings!* (Loud applause and laughter.)

Speech of Admiral David G. Farragut, U. S. Navy.

The Chairman then read the next regular toast, as follows:

"The naval ships of the United States and Great Britain: in 1858, meeting in mid-ocean, and contending together against the forces of the sea, they established a new bond of union between the two countries."

He called for a reply from the hero of New-Orleans and Mobile.

Admiral Farragut, on rising, was received with hearty cheers. He said:

Mr. President, Ladies and Gentlemen: Whilst I feel complimented by the call to respond to the sentiment which has just been read to the company, I cannot but express regret that some person more competent than myself had not been selected. (Cheers.) It was my good fortune, Mr. President, to be in this city in 1858, on the occasion of the great celebration of laying the telegraphic cable, the result, to use the words of the sentiment just offered, of the naval ships of the United States and Great Britain "meeting in mid-ocean, and contending together against the forces of the sea." (Applause.) I well remember the gratification I then felt that my fears had not been realized, and I expressed my admiration for the indefatigable energy, perseverance and skill displayed by Mr. FIELD, your honored guest, and his co-workers in the cause of science, the developments of which had in the last few years led us to believe that we knew the bottom of the ocean even better than its surface. Few, if any, Mr. President, felt more deeply interested in this wonderful, nay, most wonderful enterprise, than myself, during the entire labors of your honored guest, and no one rejoiced more in the result. And although I do not consider that our Navy had an equal share in the final contest with the elements in establishing this bond of union, yet I have an abiding faith that whenever or wherever the navies of Great Britain and the United States unite their efforts for the advancement of civilization, science or humanity, they will seldom, if ever, fail; (cheers;) and I sincerely trust that they may always be so fortunate as to receive the approbation of their fellow-countrymen as in the present case. (Cheers.) That this bond of union which now unites the two countries may never be severed, is our sincere desire; but should it chance to be, the recent skill and energy displayed by those who laid it, will be sufficient to repair and reunite it. (Loud Applause.)

SPEECH OF GEN. GEORGE G. MEADE, U. S. ARMY.

Mr. LOW said that he had been instructed to read a toast which had been unintentionally and by error omitted from the regular list. It was:

"The Army of the United States, represented by the hero of Gettysburgh." (Loud cheers.)

As General MEADE rose to reply, the cheering was renewed, and continued for some time. When quiet was restored, he said:

LADIES, AND GENTLEMEN OF THE CHAMBER OF COMMERCE: If I had been consulted I should have protested against any error having been made on this occasion. I do not see why I should have been brought before you at this particular moment. I came here after having travelled a hundred miles on a labor of love and of duty to do honor to your distinguished guest, the hero of this evening, and the only one, in my judgment, who is entitled to any consideration on this occasion. (Cheers.) I have watched with eagerness the struggle through which he has passed, and the disasters which attended his early efforts; and I have admired and applauded from the bottom of my heart the tenacity of purpose with which that man has continued to hold on to his original idea, with a firm faith to carry to completion one of the greatest works this world has ever seen. (Cheers.) I came here, therefore, to do him honor, and to show by my presence, as far as I could in my humble capacity, how much I respect him for all the qualities he has shown, which have made him not only the representative of this great city, but of our country, and, indeed, I may say of the world. (Cheers.) Now, for what you have said of the army, be pleased to accept my warmest thanks. The army requires but little from me. Its history is known to you. In a community represented by such intelligence and education as I see before me now, the deeds of this army and its record are too well known to need any recital on my part. It would be a work of supererogation. At this late hour I will say nothing of what the army has done. I will only pledge you that in the future the army will do—as in the past it always has done—its duty, (cheers,) and endeavor to uphold the honor, the integrity and the flag of our common country. (Loud cheers.)

The Chair read the next regular toast:

"Captain ANDERSON and the officers of the Great Eastern, and the other ships engaged in the late expedition—they deserve the thanks not only of their own country, but of the civilized world."

The Chairman called upon Rev. Dr. HITCHCOCK to respond.

ADDRESS OF REV. ROSWELL D. HITCHCOCK, D. D.

MR. PRESIDENT, LADIES AND GENTLEMEN: I promise you the greatest brevity in my discourse. It is now nearly 1900 years since the poet VIRGIL set sail from the eastern shore of Italy for Athens. On the eve of his departure, his friend, HORACE, indited one of his most felicitous odes, in which he inveighed against the audacity of the human race. "The strength of triple brass," he says, "must have girded about the breast of that man who first launched his frail barque on the savage sea." This, Mr. President, was not the extravagance of poetry; it was not the timidity of an uncommercial age and people. No man can go to sea in this our day, in the fastest ship, without wondering that any vessel gets safely across the tremendous expanse. No man passes through these roaring waters without admiring the heroism of every commander, of every sailor who undertakes it. It is a great thing to cross these three thousand miles of barren, tempestuous sea, and science will never annihilate the peril. Ask any experienced commander, and he will tell you he wonders so many ships keep afloat.

Horace inveighs against Prometheus, who stole fire from Heaven. I beg to know what the Roman poet would have said, had he lived in our times and found both audacities combined—the sea crossed and the lightning sent through its bosom! (Applause.)

This, I dare to say, is the most stupendous achievement in the history of our kind upon the globe; and we are to regard this achievement, not boastingly, but in all humility. The Providence of God has been with us. The "Great Eastern" was accounted a commercial blunder. It was "the wisdom of God and the power of God," in order to this great enterprise. This "commercial blunder" was necessary to its success. But for the "Great Eastern," the Atlantic cable would not now be laid. (Applause.)

In regard to the English people, before coming to Capt. Anderson, one word. I appreciate the enterprise of America in regard to all those lines of oceanic communication which American capital has set on foot; but I think no man has crossed the ocean which roars between us and England, without confessing that the English nation has surpassed all others in building ships for this purpose, fast and sure.

This Cunard line has yet sent no ship to the bottom. It has taken every man safely across. It is a grand achievement, and we must acknowledge it, to the credit of the English nation. (Applause.)

Capt. Anderson is not a man in the dull routine of English service. He is a scientific man; a well read man; he is a cultured man. I saw him first (and the only time) in the house of our friend, Mr. Field, just before he set sail on his last passage to England, intending to go in the

"Great Eastern," to lay the cable, a year ago—when it failed. Nevertheless, seeing how assured the man was, how cool, how balanced, I felt persuaded, in spite of all sceptics might say, that the thing would, at some time, somehow or other, be done. (Applause.) I felt as I did when I met Mr. FIELD in Paris—when he gave me a piece of the cable, (that he may be interested to learn I left with the Monks on St. Bernard, much to their delight)—that somehow the thing would be done; because all things are possible to faith—faith conquers all obstacles. It was the faith of Capt. ANDERSON, and the faith of Mr. FIELD, above all, that insured the success of the experiment. (Applause.)

But now I have to repeat to you one thing more about this Capt. ANDERSON, and with that I will close. He has the generosity of a sailor; and if there be in England any men, or any man, at all disposed to lessen the credit of our countryman in regard to this great enterprise, Capt. ANDERSON is not one of those men—is not that man. (Cheers.) When the cable was safely landed this summer at Heart's Content, a dinner was given on board the "Great Eastern" by Capt. ANDERSON to the officers of the telegraphic fleet, at which he said, in presence of all who had borne a part in that achievement, and who might justly feel that their own share in contributing to the general result should not be forgotten, that "he begged to congratulate all who had been engaged in the work, but no living man, in his opinion, was deserving of more credit than CYRUS W. FIELD, *to whose energy, perseverance and active exertions the world was mainly indebted for the great work now so happily terminated.*" (Applause.)

Our friend, I am persuaded, would be among the last to depreciate the share of Providence in this great work —would be among the last to lessen the just reputation of any man on the other side of the Atlantic; and yet it is due to him that we say, that the one name which could not have been dropped, without a fatal issue to the enterprise, was the name of CYRUS W. FIELD. (Applause.) Whatever other man might have been spared, this man could not have been spared. He was the *sine quâ non* of success in this grand enterprise; and we honor this robust Englishman, this honest sailor, for confessing it. (Enthusiastic cheers.)

The CHAIRMAN read the next toast:

"*The Capitalists of England and America*—who use their wealth to achieve great enterprises, and leave behind them enduring monuments of their wise munificence."

He called upon Rev. Dr. LITTLEJOHN, of Brooklyn, to respond.

ADDRESS OF REV. A. N. LITTLEJOHN, D. D.

Mr. CHAIRMAN:

Standing as I do in the presence of so many whose words would have more weight, I might be pardoned for hesitating to respond to the very important sentiment just announced. But, sir, fully persuaded that every consideration of justice and propriety demands that that sentiment should find a conspicuous place in the thoughts and associations which this occasion suggests, I shall endeavor, though with necessary brevity, to point the impressive moral which it embodies. We could not, indeed, suitably commemorate the triumph whose chief agent we are assembled to honor, and whose intrinsic greatness will make it one of the landmarks of the century, without a formal and emphatic recognition of those sagacious, large-hearted capitalists of England and America who so nobly represented in that memorable enterprise the wealth of the two countries. (Cheers.)

For, though science and the useful arts had prepared the way for it; though the prophetic instincts of two continents had ripened into a passionate hope for its achievement, yet, without wealth freely, deliberately, repeatedly ventured even to the limit, as we have heard to-night from Mr. FIELD, of sinking over twelve millions of dollars before success was attained—without wealth under the sway of an intelligence so enlarged by culture, by commerce, by love for the best interests of an advancing civilization as to grasp the world's want, and be ready to risk much to meet it—the success we celebrate to-night would have been impossible. All honor, therefore, to those whose wealth saved from failure this long-doubted, often-tried, but now historic triumph of genius over space, of character over difficulties once deemed insurmountable, of the outstretched arms of two kindred nations over the wide waste of waters rolling between them. (Applause.)

But very justly this sentiment alludes to these capitalists only as representatives of a class whom the intellect, the benevolence and the Christianity of the age are quick to discover and never reluctant to honor. It suggests many special and collateral questions of interest which I may not now be permitted to discuss. I shall not, therefore, attempt to enter into the record which the capital of our time has been making for itself, and neither shall I speak of wealth as an object of honorable ambition, nor of the unhappy extent to which it has, in many quarters, invited and justified the charges of selfishness, negligence and profligacy. Passing over these topics, I shall call attention to a more general and, in relation to this occasion, more commanding thought. By the operation of many causes, wealth has been advanced to a position of power in our modern life which renders it a question of momentous interest how, on the whole, that power will be used—by what examples, by what purposes and inspirations it will be guided. As aristocracies of blood and of royal patent wilt and wither under our nineteenth century sunlight, so that of wealth, wielded by educated intelligence, puts in a more definite and positive claim for rulership and authority. Therefore, every event, every character, every action of those whom fortune or industry and talent have placed in this class, has a special significance as showing how society is likely to be governed by this rising force.

Heretofore the accumulation of wealth has been the standing theme of our current economies. The sources whence it is derived, the laws regulating the exchanges of values, soil, climate, labor, machinery, skilled industry and kindred subjects, have been discussed and sifted until the common mind of to-day rivals in acuteness, in sagacity and general knowledge the best thinkers and educators of a generation since. But now our enormous material development and the diversified interests of society have pushed into the foreground of public thought another and more important question—the question of the right use and healthy distribution of wealth—how it shall be made tributary to the best interests of our expanding life—how it shall be brought to do the work which humanity needs and which Providence commands. Certainly there are abundant proofs of the growing subordination of the material to the moral aspects of capital. Its cold, heavy bulk begins to be penetrated and stirred by the leaven of kindlier sympathies. The soft showers of an approaching tenderness drop with genial welcome upon its ribs of iron and granite. It invites and listens with respectful interest to the discussion of problems affecting at once its safety and its duty, from which only a few years ago it would have turned in moody silence or open disgust. It begins to see God's own heralds of admonition and rebuke in the groans and tears of virtuous poverty. The moral of naked backs and empty stomachs and half sheltered bodies amid limitless abundance, it begins to understand. We, sir, are passing into a period which, to say the least, will rate the energy which heaps up, lower than the beneficent wisdom which scatters. Men that live only to fill the coffers of private selfishness—men who bury their hard-earned talent in profitless isolation—men who seize the fleeces of sheep which they have not fed, but left to wander over lonely moors—such men the large, hopeful and sympathetic spirit of our time will estimate at their true worth; nay, will find hands to plough them under as the rust and dross of a generous and humane civilization.

But happily it is laid upon me to speak of another sort of character—of men on both sides the water who will leave enduring monuments of their wise munificence, and will turn their wealth to the achievement of enterprises which in their final influence shall bless not one, but every continent of the globe. It is for these that I rise to invoke the special regard and admiration of this assembly —men who are moved by a profound sense of the duties as well as of the dignities of wealth—men who make it a conscience to believe that, as capital is the fruit of the energies, the opportunities and securities of civilization, so in turn capital should be its helper, its ornament and safeguard—men who are doing more than any thing else to redeem us from the painful and dishonoring imputation of living in an age

> Of quicken'd brains and hearts of stone,
> Which only tends to sordid ends,
> And whets the appetite for gain.

Aye, sir, men who are at work upon the stupendous moral miracle of transforming riches from the traditional root of evil into a fountain of healing waters for the ignorant, the wretched and the oppressed of every land. Such are the BRASSEYS, the PENDERS, the WORTLEYS, the ELLIOTS, the BARCLAYS, the BEWLEYS and the GOOCHS of Great Britain, with whose deeds we are more familiar than with their names. Such, too, (and I may name only a few from a list growing larger and richer every year,) are the MINTURNS, the COOPERS, the CORNELLS, the LOWS, (applause,) the DODGES, the TAYLORS, of America. Such, too —most illustrious example of all—is our own PEABODY, (applause,) (for him no plural may be used, for he has no twin name as yet on either side of the sea,) whose unparalleled munificence to the cause of charity, the cause of education and science, the tongue of envy and detraction cannot lessen. PEABODY! Sir, to use the words of a poet whose voice has just reached us from England:

Where'er that honored name is heard,
The tears will gleam in woman's eyes,
The hearts of men will stir and creep,
And blessings to their lips will rise.

Though Science joined the sundered worlds,
It needed yet what he has done;
The noblest actions, meekly wrought,
Have knit the hearts of both in one.

It is these men, and the class to which they belong, who lift capital out of the atmosphere of sordid vulgarity, and clothe it with honor. It is men of this mould who interpret and embody the true instinct of safety in the vast accumulations of living talent and industry. Their spirit, their enterprise, their endeavors to promote the public good, constitute the only shield and buckler which shall securely protect our growing wealth against the class jealousies, violences and anarchies which, sooner or later, will spring from our intense, restless, many-sided and often tumultuous democratic life. Men of this stamp, let us not question, are writing their names upon something better than pyramids, mausoleums, palaces and broad acres—the petty ambition of monarchs and conquerors—even upon the hearts of this and of coming generations. (Applause.)

England and America, long affiliated by a thousand ties of blood, literature, commerce, government and religion, but now, at last, fused into one, by the electric flame which makes the consciousness of each the living segment of a common brain: may the wealth of both be consecrated more and more to the permanent interests of a Christian civilization. (Prolonged cheers.)

The following sentiment was next read:

While expressing our grateful appreciation of the energy and sagacity that practically achieved the spanning of the Atlantic by the electric current, let us not fail to do honor to those whose genius and patient investigation of the laws of nature furnished the scientific knowledge requisite to success.

The CHAIRMAN said he had a letter from Prof. HENRY, who was assigned to respond to this toast, which was too long to read, but would be published in the proceedings. It was their duty, in this connection, also to propose the health of Prof. MORSE; for, when we revert to the history of electricity and its usefulness to mankind, we had to go back to him; and even at this late hour he would propose the health of Prof. MORSE. (Drank with applause.)

The CHAIRMAN read the following letter from Hon. WASHINGTON HUNT, Ex-Governor of New-York:

NEW-YORK, 202 FIFTH AVENUE, *Nov.* 10*th*, 1866.

GENTLEMEN:

I regret that the feeble state of my health forbids my acceptance of your invitation to meet Mr. CYRUS W. FIELD at dinner, "to exchange "congratulations on the happy result of his efforts in the great work of "uniting, by telegraph, the Old World with the New."

It would be gratifying to me to participate with you, in celebrating an event which must be regarded as the crowning achievement of an age, so remarkable for its majestic progress in inventions and improvements, calculated to promote the interests of civilization, and the welfare of mankind; and if it were possible, I would gladly join in rendering due honor to your distinguished guest, to whose enlightened energy and unconquerable perseverance we are so largely indebted, for the final consummation of this great and difficult enterprise.

By this new and wonderful agency, transmitting intelligence under mighty oceans and over the loftiest mountains, to the uttermost parts of the earth, new relations are created between the nations of the world. However remote, they are brought closely together, and united by fresh ties of interest, sympathy and peace, which cannot but exert a beneficent influence upon their future career and destiny.

While the New World is indebted to the Old, for so large a share of the arts of humanity and civilization, it is a source of just national pride, that we are enabled, in some degree, to requite the obligation, by the successful efforts of American intellect and invention. We cannot forget that the sublime instrumentality of the telegraph, by which a new light is diffused over the face of the globe, was conceived and perfected by the matchless genius and skill of one of our countrymen, whose name will be revered and honored by all the nations, during all coming time.

I remain, gentlemen, with great regard, yours truly,

WASHINGTON HUNT.

Messrs. A. A. LOW,
GEORGE OPDYKE,
WILLIAM E. DODGE,
JONATHAN STURGES,
STEWART BROWN,
SAMUEL B. RUGGLES,
Committee.

The next toast in order was

Commerce and the Atlantic Cable—prime agent and instrument of man's advancement, through accelerated intercourse between the Old World and the New.

Responded to by the Chairman of the Committee, Hon. GEORGE OPDYKE, late Mayor of the City of New-York.

SPEECH OF THE HON. GEORGE OPDYKE.

MR. PRESIDENT:

The message you have just received from Capt. ANDERSON to the honored guest on your right, which has been flashed through the wires this evening from London to the room in which we are assembled, affords ocular demonstration of the fact that *time is no longer a necessary element in the transmission of intelligence across the Atlantic.* This great truth, though now clearly established, is at once so novel and so astounding that we are as yet unprepared to realize its full significance. That its results must be most beneficent; that it will brush away, as with the magician's wand, one of the chief hindrances to the world's progress; that it will promote the commercial intercourse, the prosperity and the peace of the world, we all instinctively feel and believe. But we must await the teachings of experience before we attempt an exact portraiture of the benefits that this accelerated intercourse will confer.

The sentiment you have asked me to respond to, correctly implies that these benefits, whatever may be their extent, must be looked for chiefly through the mediation of commerce. Commerce is the great agency for promoting the social as well as the commercial intercourse of men and of nations. Its operations and its influence are world wide. It binds the human family together by a chain of inter-dependence and a community of thought. Its office is to supply the mutual wants of man by exchanging the surplus products of every individual of every nationality. In performing this service it enlarges the aggregate production of wealth by permitting the division of employments; and it widens the circle of human enjoyments by placing within the reach of all the productions of every clime. In effecting the exchange of commodities it necessarily leads to an interchange of ideas and opinions, through which knowledge is diffused, prejudices obliterated, and the race thus elevated to a higher state of civilization and refinement. (Applause.)

The usefulness of commerce is measured by the freedom and celerity of its movements. Its votaries are constantly striving for means of accelerated intercourse. To overcome the obstacles that beset its path, they have dotted the ocean with ships, and grooved the land with a labyrinth of rail-roads and canals. But these efficient auxiliaries have not satisfied the aspirations of modern commerce. In this age of mighty progress, it has longed for increased facilities in the transmission of intelligence. Thanks to the genius of Prof. MORSE and his co-laborers in physical science, it has recently been furnished, like the animal organism, with a system of nerves through which it may transmit its volitions with the quickness of thought. But until now this network of electric nerves has been bisected by the Atlantic, so that every intercontinental volition or message that reached either shore of that broad ocean, was arrested in its course and subjected to at least ten days' delay in its ferriage across. The restless spirit of commercial enterprise could not well brook such delay. But how to devise a remedy was a question not easily answered. The problem seemed as difficult of solution as any with which the human mind had ever grappled. Thanks to the distinguished gentleman whom we have met to honor, and his associates in the great enterprise, the problem has been solved; the difficulties have been met and overcome. The continental sections have been united by a spinal electric cord stretched across the bottom of the Atlantic. The electric nerves of commerce are now a unit, and co-extensive with its entire domain. Two thousand miles of watery space have been, for purposes of communication, practically condensed into as many inches, and ten days of time into as many seconds; and we now find ourselves virtually within speaking distance of all Europe. (Applause.)

Mr. President, it may appear to some that I have unduly magnified the functions of commerce, in calling the electric telegraph its nervous system. I am aware that that instrument has also its political and social uses in the transmission of diplomatic notes and messages of friendship and affection. But these are as nothing compared with those connected with commerce. A gentleman familiar with the subject informs me that the chief revenue of all our telegraphic lines is derived from despatches directly relating to commerce. If we should embrace those indirectly connected with it, and growing out of it, we should find but an infinitesimal remainder.

It is most fitting, therefore, that the Chamber of Commerce of New-York should do honor to one of its own members who, from first to last, has been the leading spirit of the great work which has placed this commercial emporium of the continent in instant communication with the whole commercial world. It is also proper, that the commercial interest, everywhere, should acknowledge its obligations to him who has been so instrumental in conferring on it, and, through it, on the world at large, this inestimable boon. In truth, all must instinctively honor the sagacity that projected, the moral courage that inaugurated, and the heroic faith that accomplished a telegraphic union of the continents—a union which cannot fail to give a quickening impulse, not merely to the interchange of ideas and products, but to the future advancement of humanity. (Applause.)

The next toast was as follows:

"Works of intercommunication by land and by sea; the distinguishing features of the nineteenth century."

The CHAIRMAN, in announcing the toast above proposed, called for an answer from Hon. SAMUEL B. RUGGLES, former President of the Board of Canal Commissioners of the State of New-York, and a Director of the Erie Railway in its early stages.

SPEECH OF HON. SAMUEL B. RUGGLES.

The nineteenth century, Mr. CHAIRMAN, begs to return you its respectful acknowledgments for the favorable view of its character presented in the sentiment just proposed. If there be aught of presumption in thus speaking in its behalf even on your kind invitation, some excuse may, perhaps, be found in the fact, that in the order of things, I was permitted to enter the world but a few weeks after the birth of the century; that I have lived with it, through its infancy, its early youth, its advancing and advanced manhood, up to this, the mellow autumn of our days. During this period, I have seen many, if not most, of its men on this side of the Atlantic, and some on the other, whose genius and energy have called into being and pushed to completion the public works of intercommunication, which have won for the century its present proud pre-eminence in the history of the world. Among these men, conspicuously stands the far-seeing, self-sustaining, indefatigable countryman of ours, that we now so gladly welcome––the civic hero, who, after years of conflict, vanquishing and enchaining the ocean, has reduced it to captivity for the service of man—the peaceful conqueror, triumphantly returning from his fifty voyages, to receive the outpouring and well-earned gratitude of his country and of the human race.

The story of this matchless victory over Nature, has been too well told this evening to need any addition, so that my remarks will be confined to one or two of the principal continental antecedents which stimulated the great achievement. I refer especially to the previous preparation by the public works on the Western and on the Eastern Continents, for the sublime conjunction which we now commemorate.

The necessity and the duty of improving and reforming the surface of the globe we inhabit, has been for ages the subject of difference and controversy.

Mankind, as a modern writer well observes, will always consist of two grand divisions, the Hopeful and the Fearful. The former school, of which our honored guest is a shining ornament, and to which I humbly claim to belong, holds the physical improvement of the outspread lands and waters committed to the care of Man by the Great Architect of Nations, which shall most vigorously and effectually evolve their dormant capacities, to be not only demanded by the highest national interests, political, pecuniary and moral, but an absolute and solemn duty, expressly enjoined by the All-wise Creator in His primeval injunction to "replenish and subdue the earth."

It was in the tender infancy of our present century, that the important secret was disclosed to Man that the waters of the globe might be practically navigated by steam. It was my privilege, in 1807, to see the first slender shallop of Robert Fulton, 16½ feet broad, and 130 feet long, partially decked, and carrying one small, but well made, engine, ascend the Hudson. Our noble river was the scene of his first success, but he saw and said that the Mississippi would behold his final and greatest triumph. Had Providence spared his precious life to the present hour, he would have seen the lineal and legitimate descendant of that little river steamboat, in the "Great Eastern," the giant steamer of the ocean, not only bearing twenty thousand tons with two thousand miles of telegraphic cable across the deep, but experimentally solving the tremendous ocean problem of strength resisting stress, and scientifically reducing the wildest commotion of the Atlantic to an algebraic equation.

It was but little more than twenty years from this first success on the Hudson, and during the early manhood of our century, that steam, the mightiest monarch of modern days, entered on its next career of conquest, in navigating the land. The railway locomotive made its first appearance on our continent in the year 1829. The camel has been figuratively, perhaps fancifully, denominated the "ship of the desert;" but is not the train of a thousand tons, swiftly drawn by the locomotive through the wilderness, with equal truth a railway "fleet" sailing with redoubled speed across the solid land? It is this fundamental transformation—this fluidifying the earth, so to speak, which imparts to the railway its transcendent continental power, and its highest political value.

It has been the steady aim during the present century of the enlightened projectors of the public works within the limits of the American Union, to render them, as far as practicable, continental in character.

As early as 1810, seven years before the Erie Canal was commenced, De Witt Clinton prophetically saw it, as Æneas saw Rome, in all its future grandeur. His eagle eye could not be limited by the narrow horizon of a single State, however imperial. He saw his State, in all its amplitude, as only the receptacle and custodian of the majestic trunk, and with equal clearness of vision he discerned the widespread and outspread branches laden with golden fruit, covering the magnificent basin of the Upper Lakes and the vast continental Valley of the Mississippi.

On the 3d of November, 1835, the first spadeful of earth was deposited at sunrise on the Erie Railway. Within the personal knowledge of some of us now here, that momentous act was then proclaimed to be the commencement of one, continuous, continental line from the Bay of New-York to the shores of the Pacific. In the thirty years which have elapsed since the birth of this great artery, it has been connected, directly or indirectly, with the whole system of American railways, now embracing a lineal extent exceeding thirty-six thousand miles,—while the interior links of the yet unfinished chain, under the Presidency of General Dix, are at this moment eagerly advancing westward and onward, to grapple with the giant ranges of snow-clad Cordilleras, kindly interposed by Providence to try our courage, between the Missouri and our Great Western Ocean.

I am well aware, that it is not the mere expenditure of money that makes either men or nations great, or which can give to centuries a just historic pre-eminence. But it nevertheless may be well to know, that the sum already actually expended in carrying forward the railways in the American Union, now exceeds thirteen hundred and eighty millions of dollars. It far transcends the total expenditure, in any preceding century, by any and all of the nations of the earth, upon any or all of their works of intercommunication. Nay, more. It actually exceeds the sum total expended by all the civilized nations known in history, whether ancient or modern,—whether for roads, or bridges, or canals, or aqueducts, or lighthouses, or artificial ports,—in the long line of eight and twenty centuries, from the reign of Solomon, the first "internal improvement" monarch of Israel, to the death of the first Napoleon, within the present century.

Nor have our neighbors across the Atlantic failed to do their duty to the age we live in. Within the same thirty years, railways of great perfection and solidity of execution, challenging comparison with the proudest works of utility in the ancient world, have made their way into the various nations of European Christendom, until the scattered links, at first disconnected, have virtually come together in one continuous European continental system, having a lineal development exceeding thirty thousand miles, and at a cost exceeding seven hundred millions of pounds sterling, or three thousand five hundred millions of dollars.

The marvellous changes wrought in both the continents, by these two great continental systems overspreading their surface, have practically transformed or reformed their whole commercial anatomy. The new arteries, with the hundreds of connecting veins opened by these capacious channels, richly filled with the vivifying blood of commerce in active circulation, have imparted new and youthful life and vigor to vast districts of interior or secluded territory, formerly inaccessible, inert or torpid, funishing cheap and convenient outlets for the products of their industry to all the lands and waters of the globe.

Not to mention the rapid increase of population, the vigorous communities called into being, the greatly increased power of locomotion of every individual, the accelerated movement of national forces, and the many other elements of political strength, the yearly saving alone in the cost of transporting persons and property, in each of the continents, is now at least five hundred millions of dollars; which immense amount, annually swelling, must roll onward and upward for generations to come.

But what, after all, was the power of saving even these enormous sums in the transportation over the continents of gross material products in persons and property, compared with the higher, more intellectual, more ethereal office of expediting and cheapening the transmission of intelligence and thought throughout their wide expanse? Teeming as they were with the added wealth set in such animated motion, had not the electric telegraph become an immediate, an absolute, a world-wide necessity? Had not the time arrived, for our own MORSE to appear? Was it not the very hour for the genius of the nineteenth century to wave his wand, and evoke from the deep sleep of Nature that mysterious power, by whose subtle agency time and space might be annihilated?

The first slender telegraphic wire, with a petty electric apparatus in the Capitol, was put up by MORSE between Washington and Baltimore in 1844. Within twenty years, it ramified through all the States of the American Union, and crossing the mountains and plains of the great interior, was looking out on the Pacific. Its lines, ninety thousand miles in length, under the powerful attraction of the neighboring Russian Empire, so eloquently depicted this evening, were stretching up the Pacific coast and under the polar circle, to reach, by an immense continental circuit of nearly ten thousand miles, the Oriental and Southern nations of Asia. Europe was also vivified by a connected net-work of wires exceeding sixty thousand miles in length, transmitting its varied and multiform intelligence, with lightning speed, to its Atlantic coast. Continental distance on land had ceased to exist, but a yawning gulf in the deep abyss of the Atlantic yet remained to separate the Hemispheres.

Such, then, were the continental antecedents which led our honored guest to enter on his long and arduous, but, thanks be to God, his victorious career. He found the Continents mutually glowing with the fervor of their rich and newly awakened commerce, gazing wishfully at each other across this ocean gulf. Marriage had become indispensable. Our distinguished guest was the "Friar Lawrence," who "made" them "incorporate, two in one."

This difficult achievement in thus uniting the continents was no random performance,—no merely fortunate hit,—no lucky groping in the dark. So far from that, the animated narrative of the voyages of our benefactor, destined to live in historic literature with the story of Columbus, shows him incessantly holding up the lamp of science, not only guiding his path to sure success, but pointing out the way for all the world to follow. This it is, which lends to his great success its highest, its truly world-wide value. The geographical delineation of the dark and hitherto unfathomed ocean floor, with its myriads of microscopic occupants obediently coming up to reveal the topography of their deep resting-place—the accuracy, delicacy and exquisite efficiency of the electric apparatus—the mathematical demonstration accurately establishing the rate of speed for the giant steamer, consistent with the safety of the telegraphic cable—all these weapons of thought, so potent in winning this great victory over Nature, he now presents not alone to his patriotic band of monied associates, to whom all honor be rendered, but to all the governments and peoples of the civilized world. If COLUMBUS, in the words of his epitaph, "gave a new world to Castile and Leon," our cosmopolitan countryman has furnished to both the worlds, the precious scientific knowledge needed for binding themselves forever in harmonious conjunction.

Here, then, we pause. We have lived to see but a portion of the wondrous epic of the nineteenth century. The rest is yet to come. But some of us now here will live to see its close, with a free and intelligent population of a hundred millions busy with the glorious lands and waters of the American Union, "now and forever one and indivisible." They will then behold the whole available bed of the Atlantic brought by full and careful surveys to geographical certainty, enchained or enslaved by no single work, but striped with cables at all proper and convenient intervals uniting the nations of Western Europe with the American coast, and reducing to the lowest practicable minimum the cost of daily and hourly intercommunication between the Continents—and they may also behold regenerated Africa holding close communion with all its emancipated brethren in the Western Hemisphere, whether north or south of the Equator. Then will our nineteenth century, already so rich with well-directed efforts, so pregnant with sublime results, fill up its fullest measure of historic fame—then may it lie contentedly and confidently down in the common grave of the buried ages, and leave its great example for the guidance and encouragement of all who may follow "to the last syllable of recorded Time." (Applause.)

The CHAIRMAN read the two following toasts, to which there was no time for reply:

The City of New-York—The front door of the New World, whose bell-pull is now on the cliffs of Valentia.

The Cable and the Press.—Emitting light from the sea, and spreading it abroad—they illuminate the world.

The former of these was to have been responded to by Hon. JOHN T. HOFFMAN, Mayor of the City of New-York, and the latter by the Rev. HENRY WARD BEECHER; but in consequence of the lateness of the hour these gentlemen had departed to their homes.

The CHAIRMAN said, the last toast on the list was THE LADIES:

Who, oh who, with woman near,
  Forgets not earth and its every thrall;
Oh! who but feels that woman dear,
  Though last, was the crowning gift of all!

(Drank all standing.)

A vote of thanks was passed to Messrs. WILLIAM T. BLODGETT, MARSHALL LEFFERTS, WILLIAM E. DODGE, JR., LOUIS LANG, RICHARD M. HUNT, JAMES LORIMER GRAHAM, JR., and GEORGE WILSON, Committee of Arrangements, to which Mr. LOUIS LANG made a brief response. Referring to the artistic decorations of the room, which represented the earth as in telegraphic communication with the sun and moon, he said he had communicated with the celestial bodies, (he could not tell the secret how,) and engaged them to take part in the exercises. This explained the failure of the meteoric display, that had been announced.

There could be no shower; for they were all "booked on" here. (Laughter.)

Mr. Opdyke: I have a single motion to make, and it is a vote of thanks to the Chairman of the evening, for the able and courteous manner in which he has presided over this festival. You will feel it is eminently his due, when I state that for a whole week his time has been engrossed by correspondence and other duties incident to this occasion.

Carried, with warm applause.

The band then played a parting air, and the company slowly retired, having enjoyed an evening long to be remembered.

INVITED GUESTS PRESENT.

Hon. LAFAYETTE S. FOSTER, Acting Vice-President of the United States.

Admiral DAVID G. FARRAGUT, U. S. Navy.
Major-General GEORGE G. MEADE. U. S. Army.
Rear-Admiral CHARLES H. BELL, U. S. Navy.
Commodore CADWALADER RINGGOLD, U. S. Navy.
Captain ALEXANDER M. PENNOCK, U. S. Navy.
General WILLIAM F. SMITH, U. S. Army.
H. E. Senhor D'AZAMBUJA, Minister from Brazil.
H. E. DOMINGO FAUSTINO SARMIENTO, Minister of the Argentine Rep.
GAULDREE BOILLEAU, Esq., Consul-General for France.
C. EDWARD HABICHT, Esq., Consul-General for Sweden.

Hon. JOHN T. HOFFMAN, Mayor of New-York City.

Hon. STEPHEN J. FIELD, Judge of the Supreme Court of the United States.
Hon. HENRY E. DAVIES, Judge of Court of Appeals of New-York.
Hon. DANIEL P. INGRAHAM, Judge Supreme Court of New-York.
Hon. JOSIAH SUTHERLAND, " " " "
Hon. THOMAS W. CLERKE, " " " "
Hon. ANTHONY L. ROBERTSON, Judge Superior Court "
Hon. CLAUDIUS L. MONELL, " " " "
Hon. JOHN M. BARBOUR, " " " "
Hon. SAMUEL JONES, " " " "
Hon. JOHN H. McCUNN, " " " "
Hon. CHARLES P. DALY, Judge Court Common Pleas, "
Hon. JOHN R. BRADY, " " " " "
Hon. RICHARD O'GORMAN.
Hon. HORACE GREELEY.
Hon. HENRY J. RAYMOND.
Hon. JAMES BROOKS.
Hon. GEORGE BANCROFT.
Hon. EZRA CORNELL.
Hon. JOHN JAY.
Hon. DAVID A. WELLS.

Most Rev. JOHN McCLOSKEY, Archbishop of New-York.
Rev. WILLIAM ADAMS, D. D.
Rev. HENRY W. BELLOWS, D. D.
Rev. STEPHEN H. TYNG, D. D.
Rev. ROSWELL D. HITCHCOCK, D. D.
Rev. SAMUEL OSGOOD, D. D.
Rev. HENRY M. FIELD, D. D.
Rev. THOMAS E. VERMILYE, D. D.
Rev. HENRY WARD BEECHER.
Rev. JOSEPH T. DURYEA, D. D.
Rev. A. N. LITTLEJOHN, D. D.
Rev. THOMAS DE WITT, D. D.
Rev. GEORGE L. PRENTISS, D. D.
Rev. EDWARD A. WASHBURN, D. D.
Rev. JAMES G. CRAIGHEAD.

FREDERICK A. P. BARNARD, LL. D., President Columbia College.
MARK HOPKINS, LL. D., President Williams College, Mass.
HORACE WEBSTER, LL. D., President New-York Free College.
ISAAC FERRIS, LL. D., President New-York University.
Rev. JOHN MacLEAN, D. D., President Princeton College.
ALONZO CRITTENDEN, LL. D., Principal Packer Institute, Brooklyn.
DAVID H. COCHRAN, LL. D., Principal Polytechnic Institute, "
Professor THEODORE W. DWIGHT, LL. D.
FRANCIS LIEBER, LL. D.
Professor J. E. HILGARD, of the Coast Survey, Washington.
Dr. ISAAC I. HAYES, of the Arctic Expedition.

CHARLES O'CONOR, Esq.
WILLIAM M. EVARTS, Esq.
CHARLES A. DANA, Esq.
DAVID M. STONE, Esq.
CHESTER P. DEWEY, Esq.
SIDNEY E. MORSE, Jr., Esq.
FRANK LESLIE, Esq.
EDWARD CARY, Esq.
CHARLES NORDHOFF, Esq.
JAMES TINKER, Esq.
HENRY E. PIERREPONT, Esq.
J. CARSON BREVOORT, Esq.
FREDERICK DE PEYSTER, Esq.
HOWARD POTTER, Esq.
PROSPER M. WETMORE, Esq.
JOSHUA M. VAN COTT, Esq.
O. H. PALMER, Esq.
R. N. McALPINE, Esq.
JAMES LORIMER GRAHAM, Jr., Esq.
LOUIS LANG, Esq.

PERRY McDONOUGH COLLINS, Es
THOMAS WALSH, Esq.
THOMAS T. ECKERT, Esq.
ALFRED BIERSTADT, Esq.
EMANUEL LEUTZE, Esq.
LE VICOMTE CHORBAL.
AUGUSTUS E. MASTERS, Esq.
RICHARD M. HUNT, Esq.
WILLIAM E. EVERETT, Esq.
CHARLES FORSTMAN, Esq.
Captain EDWARD G. LOTT.
HIRAM SIBLEY, Esq.
JOHN HORNER, Esq.
DUDLEY FIELD, Esq.
WILLIAM F. JUDSON, Esq.
CHARLES GOOCH, Esq.
CHARLES P. KIRKLAND, Esq.
CAMBRIDGE LIVINGSTON, Esq.
THOMAS McELRATH, Esq.
R. W. LOWBER, Esq.
JOHN CROSBY BROWN, Esq.
CHARLES D. DICKEY, Esq.
CHARLES L. TIFFANY, Esq.
THOMAS C. ACTON, Esq.
JOHN A. KENNEDY, Esq.
RICHARD GRANT WHITE, Esq.

CORRESPONDENCE.

THE following are among the letters received by the committee in reply to the card of invitation:

Letter from the President of the United States.

EXECUTIVE MANSION,
WASHINGTON, D. C., *Nov.* 10, 1866.

GENTLEMEN:

I have received your invitation to meet Mr. CYRUS W. FIELD at a dinner to be given by the Chamber of Commerce of New-York, on the 15th instant, for the purpose of exchanging "congratulations on the happy result of his efforts in the great work of uniting by telegraph the Old World with the New," and regret that the pressure of public business will not permit me to join you in doing honor to the eminent citizen whose name is so inseparably connected with that great achievement.

I am, gentlemen,
Very respectfully yours,
ANDREW JOHNSON.

Messrs. A. A. LOW,
GEORGE OPDYKE,
WM. E. DODGE and others,
Committee of the Chamber of Commerce, New-York.

Letter from Hon. SALMON P. CHASE, *Chief Justice of the United States.*

WASHINGTON, *Nov.* 13, 1866.

GENTLEMEN:

I am very sorry that I cannot leave Washington this week, and so cannot avail myself of your kind invitation to join you in congratulation to Mr. FIELD upon the success of his grand undertaking. It is the most wonderful achievement of civilization; and to his sagacity, patience, perseverance, courage and faith is civilization indebted for it.

New-York, already the greatest city of America, and destined to become the greatest city of the world, honors herself by honoring a citizen so deserving and so distinguished. His success has brought her commerce within hail of every considerable port in Europe. The Atlantic Telegraph, his work, in connexion with the Russian American Telegraph, originated by another citizen of your State, will make the merchants of New-York next door neighbors to all the merchants of the earth.

Such works entitle their authors to distinguished rank among public benefactors. You will write the name of your honored guest high upon that illustrious roll, and there it will remain in honor, while oceans divide and Telegraphs unite mankind.

Yours, very respectfully,
S. P. CHASE.

Messrs. A. A. LOW,
GEORGE OPDYKE,
WM. E. DODGE,
JONATHAN STURGES,
STEWART BROWN,
SAMUEL B. RUGGLES,
Committee of Chamber of Commerce, New-York.

Letter from Hon. EDWIN M. STANTON, *Secretary of War.*

WAR DEPARTMENT, WASHINGTON CITY,
November 8, 1866.

GENTLEMEN:

I have the honor to acknowledge the receipt of your invitation to meet Mr. CYRUS W. FIELD at dinner, on the 15th instant, and regret my inability to be present on that occasion.

Your obedient servant,
EDWIN M. STANTON.

Messrs. A. A. LOW,
GEORGE OYDYKE, &c.,
Committee of Chamber of Commerce.

Letter from Hon. GIDEON WELLES, *Secretary of the Navy.*

WASHINGTON, D. C., *November* 13, 1866.

GENTLEMEN:

I am honored with your invitation to meet Mr. CYRUS W. FIELD at dinner, on the 15th instant, to exchange congratulations on the happy result of his efforts in the great work of uniting by Telegraph the Old World with the New.

I shall be happy on all occasions to participate in awarding honors to the indomitable energy, personal worth, and public services of Mr. FIELD, but shall be unable to be present with you on the 15th instant.

With special regards to him, to the Chamber of Commerce of the State of New-York, and to yourselves, individually,

I am, very respectfully,

GIDEON WELLES.

Messrs. A. A. LOW,
GEORGE OPDYKE,
WM. E. DODGE,
JONATHAN STURGES,
STEWART BROWN,
SAMUEL B. RUGGLES,
Committee.

Letter from Hon. HUGH MCCULLOCH, *Secretary of the Treasury.*

TREASURY DEPARTMENT, *Nov.* 8, 1866.

GENTLEMEN:

My official duties will not permit me to accept your kind invitation to meet Mr. CYRUS W. FIELD at dinner, at the Metropolitan Hotel, on the 15th instant.

I regard it an honor to be invited to join my fellow-citizens in New-York, in paying honor to one whose name will be forever associated with the great enterprise of the age, the success of which is to be attributed mainly to his strong faith and wonderful persistency. The people of the United States have reason to be proud of Mr. FIELD, and they are proud of him. I am pleased to know that you propose to give expression to the public sentiment in a manner that cannot fail to be gratifying to him and honorable to New-York.

I am, very truly,
Your obedient servant,
HUGH McCULLOCH.

Messrs. A. A. LOW,
GEORGE OPDYKE,
WM. E. DODGE,
JONATHAN STURGES,
STEWART BROWN,
SAMUEL B. RUGGLES,
Committee, New-York.

Letter from General U. S. GRANT, *U. S. Army.*

HEADQUARTERS ARMIES OF THE UNITED STATES,
WASHINGTON, D. C., Nov. 8, 1866.

GENTLEMEN:

Your kind invitation to me to meet Mr. CYRUS W. FIELD at dinner on the 15th inst., to exchange congratulations on the success of the great enterprise which has engaged so much of his time for some years, is received. It would afford me great pleasure to be able to accept, but I fear other engagements will prevent. Allow me, however, to express my appreciation of the enterprise which Mr. FIELD has been engaged in, and to congratulate him upon the success which finally was attained through his perseverance.

I have the honor to be,
With great respect,
Your obedient servant,
U. S. GRANT,
General.

To A. A. Low and Gentlemen of Committee.

Letter from Hon. JOHN A. DIX, *Minister to France.*

NEW-YORK, *Nov.* 14, 1866.

GENTLEMEN:

It is with sincere regret that I find myself unable to accept your invitation to meet Mr. CYRUS W. FIELD at dinner to-morrow, and exchange congratulations with him on the happy result of his efforts to unite by telegraph the Old World and the New. The whole commercial community—and, I may add, the whole community of nations—owe him a debt of gratitude which cannot well be repaid. He has not only exhibited extraordinary genius in carrying out the great enterprise of which he has been the chief promoter and agent, but he has displayed that which is often better than genius, a steady and determined persistence, which no obstacle or discouragement could overcome. I am most happy to unite with you—though I cannot do so personally—in the expression of my respect for his energy and perseverance, and my gratification at a success so triumphant for him and so beneficial to mankind, by facilitating the intercommunication of intelligence and thought.

I am, very respectfully yours,

John A. Dix.

Messrs. A. A. Low,
George Opdyke,
Wm. E. Dodge,
Jonathan Sturges,
Stewart Brown,
Samuel B. Ruggles, } *Committee.*

Letter from Vice-Admiral David D. Porter, *U. S. Navy.*

U. S. Naval Academy, Annapolis, Md., *Nov.* 7, 1866.

Gentlemen: I have received your polite invitation to meet Mr. Cyrus W. Field at dinner on the 15th, "to exchange congratulations on the happy result of his efforts in uniting by telegraph the Old and New Worlds."

It would give me great pleasure to accept your invitation, but the pressure of my official duties will prevent my attendance.

I am, gentlemen, very respectfully,
Your obedient servant,

David D. Porter,
Vice-Admiral and Sup't N. A.

Messrs. A. A. Low,
Geo. Opdyke,
Wm. E. Dodge and others, *Committee.*

Letter from His Excellency Sir Frederick Bruce, *Envoy Extraordinary and Minister Plenipotentiary from Great Britain at Washington.*

British Legation, Washington, *Nov.* 8, 1866.

Sir Frederick Bruce has the honor to acknowledge the receipt of the invitation to be present at the dinner given to Mr. FIELD on the completion of the Atlantic Telegraph. He would gladly have attended at the tribute so justly paid to the energy and exertion of Mr. FIELD in carrying through this great enterprise, but his engagements put it out of his power to leave Washington at present.

To the Committee, Chamber of Commerce, New-York.

Letter from His Excellency Senor M. ROMERO, *Envoy Extraordinary and Minister Plenipotentiary for Mexico at Washington.*

LEGACION MEXICANA EN LOS E. UNIDOS DE AMERICA,
WASHINGTON, *November 7th,* 1866.

GENTLEMEN:

I had the honor of receiving this morning the invitation with which the Chamber of Commerce of the State of New-York favored me, to meet Mr. CYRUS W. FIELD at dinner, on Thursday, the 15th instant, at six o'clock, P. M., at the Metropolitan Hotel, in the City of New-York, to exchange congratulations on the happy result of his efforts in the great work of uniting by telegraph the Old World with the New.

It would afford me, gentlemen, very great pleasure were I allowed to do so, to participate in that significant demonstration with which the great City of New-York celebrates one of the most extraordinary and useful feats of human skill and perseverance. But, unfortunately, my public duties at this critical period for my country will not permit me to leave Washington for the present.

I most heartily congratulate the merchants of New-York who have contributed so much to the success of that enterprise in which the Government and people of Mexico have so deep an interest, hoping soon to be able to fully reap its advantages.

I am, gentlemen, with high respect,
Your most obedient servant,

M. ROMERO.

Messrs. A. A. LOW,
GEORGE OPDYKE,
WM. E. DODGE,
JONATHAN STURGES,
STEWART BROWN,
SAMUEL B. RUGGLES,
Committee of Invitation of the New-York Chamber of Commerce, New York City.

Letter from Hon. E. D. MORGAN, *of the United States Senate.*

NEW-YORK, *November* 13, 1866.

GENTLEMEN:

I have had the honor to receive your invitation to meet Mr. CYRUS W FIELD at dinner on Thursday next, to exchange congratulations on the happy result of his efforts in the great work of constructing the Atlantic Telegraph.

I shall be deprived the pleasure of accepting the invitation, but this compliment to Mr. FIELD is most richly deserved; for if there is any one man to whom, more than to any other, and to all others combined, the country is indebted for having been chiefly instrumental in uniting by telegraph through mid-ocean "the Old World with the New," that man is CYRUS W. FIELD.

The fire that he kindled, and which now runs from shore to shore, will illuminate both continents, and by its bright light, nations, as well as individuals, will be conducted to a higher degree of civilization, and to a greater progress.

No one, then, need be surprised at an outburst of gratitude to the individual who had the genius to conceive this magnificent but perilous undertaking, and the courage and determination to continue in it to the end.

All honor to Mr. FIELD, the author and projector of the "Atlantic Cable," and honor to the Chamber of Commerce for their compliment to their fellow-citizen.

And now, gentlemen, let us use this cable; use it often and freely, by day and by night, in our public affairs, in our social relations and for commercial purposes. None can estimate or anticipate how largely our interests will be promoted by doing so. Besides, in no other way can we so practically and sufficiently compliment and remunerate its originator for the untold benefit he has conferred upon mankind.

I have the honor to be,
With great esteem,
Your obedient servant,
E. D. MORGAN.

To Messrs. A. A. LOW,
GEORGE OPDYKE,
WILLIAM E. DODGE and others, *Committee.*

Letter from Hon. CHARLES SUMNER, *of the United States Senate.*

BOSTON, *November* 14, 1866.

GENTLEMEN :

I regret much that it is not in my power to unite with you in tribute to Mr. FIELD, according to the invitation with which you have honored me.

There are events which can never be forgotten in the history of civilization. Conspicuous among these was the discovery of the New World by CHRISTOPHER COLUMBUS. And now a kindred event is added to the list. The two worlds are linked together.

In this work Mr. FIELD has been pioneer and discoverer. As such his name will be remembered with that gratitude which is bestowed upon the world's benefactors. Already his fame has begun.

Accept my thanks, and believe me, gentlemen,

Faithfully yours,

CHARLES SUMNER.

To Committee, &c.

Letter from Prof. JOSEPH HENRY, *Secretary of the Smithsonian Institution.*

SMITHSONIAN INSTITUTION, WASHINGTON, *Nov.* 12, 1866.

To the Committee of the Chamber of Commerce, New-York:

GENTLEMEN :

I have delayed acknowledging the receipt of your kind invitation to be present at the congratulatory dinner to be given to Mr. CYRUS W. FIELD, on account of the success of his labors in joining the Old and the New World in electrical sympathy, hoping to be able to accept it, but I have now to regret that I find it incompatible with previous engagements to be in New-York at the time specified.

I beg to assure you that I highly appreciate the honor of the invitation, and that it would be a source of gratification to be present on the occasion, and to offer Mr. FIELD in person my heartfelt congratulations on the happy termination of his persevering efforts to accomplish an object so intimately connected with the advance of humanity.

Science having developed the principles, and *art* having devised the means for the practical accomplishment of the desired end, there was still wanting a man of enthusiastic temperament, enlarged views as to the importance of the object, persuasive powers to convince others, business talents of high order, persevering industry and indomitable energy. All these requisites have been found happily blended in Mr. CYRUS W. FIELD, and he has been the chosen one to complete an enterprise which marks an epoch in the history of civilization.

Mr. FIELD has not in his unparalleled efforts been actuated by the mere hope of pecuniary gain, but by that cherished feeling of a noble mind, the desire to deserve and obtain the approbation of his fellow-men—to honorably connect his name with history, and to live in the memory of the good when he shall have finished his career upon earth.

Such an incentive to action is allied to our higher moral nature, springs from our instincts of immortality, and should in all cases of its manifestation be cherished and encouraged.

It is therefore abundantly proper, that Mr. FIELD should receive the cordial greetings of his friends and the public, and that the Government itself should bestow upon him marks of its approbation. Such demonstrations are not only proper in themselves, but are even expedient, if we allow a motive of this kind to influence our acts; they serve to stimulate others to similar efforts, and tend to increase the good and diminish the evil incident to our present condition.

In conclusion, permit me to say, that I have more pleasure in expressing these sentiments in regard to Mr. FIELD, than I would have in embracing the opportunity you have so kindly given me, of speaking of my own early labors in regard to the telegraph. The associations connected with these are not those of unalloyed pleasure, and I would prefer to leave it to history to make the proper award, than to say any thing myself which might call forth discussion.

I am, very respectfully,

Your obedient servant,

JOSEPH HENRY.

Letter from THOMAS HILL, LL. D., *President of Harvard College.*

CAMBRIDGE, MASS., *November* 13, 1866.

GENTLEMEN:

I much regret to find myself compelled to forego the pleasure of meeting the Chamber of Commerce and invited guests, to exchange congratulations with each other, and with Mr. FIELD on the success of the great work of uniting by telegraph the Old World with the New. Believe me, I am not insensible to the honor of receiving your invitation, nor indifferent to the fact that the ocean no longer separates, but now unites the nations; and through those abysses which heathen fancy peopled with uncouth divinities, christian hands have made a highway for christian thought and speech.

Very sincerely yours,

THOMAS HILL.

To Messrs. A. A. LOW,
GEORGE OPDYKE,
WM. E. DODGE,
JONATHAN STURGES,
STEWART BROWN,
SAMUEL B. RUGGLES, } *Committee.*

Letter from GEORGE PEABODY, ESQ.

ZANESVILLE, OHIO, *November 8th*, 1866.

GENTLEMEN:

I sincerely regret that I cannot be present at the dinner you propose to give on Thursday, the 15th inst., in honor to CYRUS W. FIELD, on the successful laying of the Atlantic Telegraph Cable. The industry, perseverance and ability which Mr. FIELD has evinced for ten years past to bring this great work to a successful result, entitle him to great praise.

Very respectfully and truly yours,

GEORGE PEABODY.

To A. A. Low and others.

Letter from BAYARD TAYLOR, ESQ.

KENNETT SQUARE, PEORIA, ILL., *November* 12, 1866.

GENTLEMEN:

To my very great regret, engagements previously made prevent me from accepting your kind invitation.

I had the good fortune to be a guest and companion of Mr. Field on the coast of Newfoundland, in the summer of 1855, when the first attempt was made to lay a submarine cable across the Gulf of St. Lawrence. During that voyage I learned to appreciate his wonderful patience, energy and courage, and no one of his friends can more rejoice in the final triumph which these qualities have achieved for him. I was in Germany when the success of the first transatlantic cable seemed to be assured, and at that time contributed to the newspapers there an account of the enterprise, in which I claimed for Mr. Field the credit which the European editors then gave exclusively to his English associates. I am convinced that if any great undertaking was ever due to the will and the faith of a single man, then the honor of having connected Europe and America by telegraph belongs to Cyrus W. Field.

I have the honor to be, gentlemen,

Very respectfully yours,

Bayard Taylor.

To Messrs. A. A. Low,
George Opdyke,
Wm. E. Dodge,
Jonathan Sturges,
Stewart Brown,
Samuel B. Ruggles, } *Committee.*

Letter from Hon. Gulian C. Verplanck.

New-York, 14*th November*, 1866.

G. C. Verplanck returns his sincere thanks to the Chamber of Commerce for the kind invitation to meet Mr. Cyrus W. Field, on the 15th inst., to exchange congratulations on the grand results of his arduous labors in uniting the Old World with the New by telegraph. Mr. Verplanck cordially joins in the wide and warm demonstrations of public gratitude, of which the Chamber of Commerce of New-York is the most appropriate and honorable representative.

But circumstances beyond his control oblige him reluctantly to decline this pleasing and flattering invitation.

His absence from the city, until last evening, must be his apology for his delay in replying to the invitation.

Telegram from His Excellency HASTINGS DOYLE, *Lieutenant-Governor of New-Brunswick.*

FREDERICTON, N. B.,
November 22, 1866.

CYRUS W. FIELD, Esq.,
New-York:

A card of invitation to meet you at dinner on the fifteenth instant, has only this day (twenty-second) reached me from Canada with Lord MONCK's signature at the corner of the envelope. Had I received it in due time, although it would have been inconvenient, I would have gone to assist in doing you that honor you so richly deserve. Pray accept my great regret at this *contretemps*, and believe in the sincerity of my friendship and admiration of your indomitable pluck.

HASTINGS DOYLE,
Major General and Administrator
of Government of New-Brunswick.

www.ingramcontent.com/pod-product-compliance
Lightning Source LLC
LaVergne TN
LVHW011119110826
845150LV00008B/2187

* 9 7 8 1 4 2 5 5 0 6 5 8 2 *